REVOLUTION AND
COUNTER - REVOLUTION

OR

GERMANY IN 1848

BY
KARL MARX

Edited by ELEANOR MARX AVELING

Martino Publishing
Mansfield Centre, CT
2014

Martino Publishing
P.O. Box 373,
Mansfield Centre, CT 06250 USA

ISBN   978-161427-6-326

© *2014 Martino Publishing*

Cover design by T. Matarazzo

Printed in the United States of America On 100% Acid-Free Paper

REVOLUTION AND
COUNTER - REVOLUTION

OR

GERMANY IN 1848

BY

KARL MARX

Edited by ELEANOR MARX AVELING

CHICAGO
CHARLES H. KERR & COMPANY

NOTE BY THE EDITOR

The following articles are now, after forty-five years, for the first time collected and printed in book form. They are an invaluable pendant to Marx's work on the *coup d'état* of Napoleon III. ("Der Achtzehnte Brumaire des Louis Bonaparte.") Both works belong to the same period, and both are what Engels calls "excellent specimens of that marvellous gift . . . of Marx . . . of apprehending clearly the character, the significance, and the necessary consequences of great historical events at a time when these events are actually in course of taking place, or are only just completed."

These articles were written in 1851-1852, when Marx had been about eighteen months in England. He was living with his wife, three young children, and their life-long friend, Helene Demuth, in two rooms in Dean Street, Soho, almost opposite the Royalty Theatre. For nearly ten years they had been driven from pillar to post. When, in 1843, the Prussian Government suppressed the *Rhenish Gazette* which Marx had edited, he went with his newly-married wife, Jenny von Westphalen, to Paris. Not long after, his expulsion was demanded by the **Prussian** Government—it is said that Alexander von Humboldt acted as the agent of Prussia on this occasion—and M. Guizot was, of course, too polite to refuse the request. Marx was expelled, and betook himself to Brussels. Again the Prussian Government requested his expulsion, and where the French Government had complied it was not likely the Belgian would refuse. Marx received marching orders.

But at this same time the French Government that had expelled Marx had gone the way of French Governments, and the new Provisional Government through Ferdinand Flocon invited the "brave et loyal Marx" to return to the country whence "tyranny had banished him, and where he, like all fighting in the sacred cause, the cause of the fraternity of all peoples," would be welcome. The invitation was accepted, and for some months he lived in Paris. Then he returned to Germany in order to start the *New Rhenish Gazette* in Cologne. And the *Rhenish Gazette* writers had very lively times. Marx was twice prosecuted, but as the juries would not convict, the Prussian Government took the nearer way and suppressed the paper.

Again Marx and his family returned to the country whose "doors" had only a few short months before been "thrown open" to him. The sky had changed—and the Government. "We remained in Paris," my mother says in some biographical notes I have found, "a month. Here also there was to be no resting-place for us. One fine morning the familiar figure of the sergeant of police appeared with the announcement that Karl 'et sa dame' must leave Paris within twenty-four hours. We were graciously told we might be interned at Vannes in the Morbihan. Of course we could not accept such an exile as that, and I again gathered together my small belongings to seek a safe haven in London. Karl had hastened thither before us." The "us" were my mother, Helene Demuth, and the three little children, Jenny (Madame Longuet), Laura (Madame Lafargue), and Edgar, who died at the age of eight.

The haven was safe indeed. But it was storm-tossed. Hundreds of refugees—all more or less destitute—were now in London. There followed years of horrible poverty, of bitter suffering—such suffering as can only be known to the penniless stranger in a strange land. The misery would have been unendurable but for the faith that was in these men and women, and but for their invincible "Humor." I use the German word because I know no English one that quite expresses the same thing—such a combination of humor and good-humor, of light-hearted courage, and high spirits.

That readers of these articles may have some idea of the conditions under which Marx was working, under which he wrote them and the "Achtzehnte Brumaire," and was preparing his first great economical work, "Zur Kritik der Politischen Oeconomie" (published in 1859), I again quote from my mother's notes. Soon after the arrival of the family a second son was born. He died when about two years old. Then a fifth child, a little girl, was born. When about a year old, she too fell sick and died. "Three days," writes my mother, "the poor child wrestled with death. She suffered so... Her little dead body lay in the small back room; we all of us" (i. e., my parents, Helene Demuth, and the three elder children) "went into the front room, and when night came we made us beds on the floor, the three living children lying by us. And we wept for the little angel resting near us, cold and dead. The death of the dear child came in the time of our bitterest poverty. Our German friends could not help us; Engels, after vainly trying to get literary work in London, had been obliged to go, under very disadvantageous conditions, into his father's firm, as a clerk, in Manchester; Ernest Jones, who often came to see us at this time, and had promised help, could do nothing.... In the anguish of my heart I went to a French refugee who lived near, and who had sometimes visited us. I told him our sore need. At once with the friendliest kindness he gave me £2. With that we paid for the little coffin in which the poor child now sleeps peacefully. I had no cradle for her when she was born, and even the last small resting-place was long denied her.".... "It was a terrible time," Liebknecht writes to me (the Editor), "but it was grand nevertheless."

In that "front room" in Dean Street, the children playing about him, Marx worked. I have heard tell how the children would pile up chairs behind him to represent a coach, to which he was harnessed as horse, and would "whip him up" even as he sat at his desk writing.

Marx ha1 been recommended to Mr. C. A. Dana,* the managing director of the *New York Tribune*, by Ferdinand Freiligrath, and the first contributions sent by him to America are the series of letters on Germany here reprinted. They seem to have created such a sensation that before the series had been completed Marx was engaged as regular London correspondent. On the 12th of March, 1852, Mr. Dana wrote: "It may perhaps give you pleasure to know that they" (i. e., the "Germany" letters) "are read with satisfaction by a considerable number of persons, and are widely reproduced." From this time on, with short intervals, Marx not only sent letters regularly to the New York paper; he wrote a large number of leading articles for it. "Mr. Marx," says an editorial note in 1853, "has indeed opinions of his own, with some of which we are far from agreeing; but those who do not read his letters neglect one of the most instructive sources of information on the great questions of European politics."

Not the least remarkable among these contributions were those dealing with Lord Palmerston and the Russian Government. "Urquhart's writings on Russia," says Marx, "had interested but

---

* Mr. C. A. Dana was at this time still in sympathy with Socialism. The effects of Brook Farm had not yet worn off.

not convinced me. In order to arrive at a definite opinion, I made a minute analysis of Hansard's Parliamentary Debates, and of the Diplomatic Blue Books from 1807 to 1850. The first fruits of these studies was a series of articles in the *New York Tribune,* in which I proved Palmerston's relations with the Russian Government. ... Shortly after, these studies were reprinted in the Chartist organ edited by Ernest Jones, *The People's Paper*... Meantime the Glasgow *Sentinel* had reproduced one of these articles, and part of it was issued in pamphlet form by Mr. Tucker, London." * And the Sheffield Foreign Affairs Committee thanked Marx for the "great public service rendered by the admirable *exposé"* in his "Kars papers," published both in the *New York Tribune* and the *People's Paper*. A large number of articles on the subject were also printed in the *Free Press* by Marx's old friend, C. D. Collett. I hope to republish these and other articles.

As to the *New York Tribune,* it was at this time an admirably edited paper, with an immense staff of distinguished contributors,† both American and European. It was a passionate anti-slavery organ, and also recognized that there "was need for a true organization of society," and that "our evils" were "social, not political." The paper, and especially Marx's articles, were

---

* "Herr Vogt," pp. 59 and 185. London, 1860.
† Including Bruno Bauer, Bayard Taylor, Ripley, and many of the Brook Farmers. The editor was Horace Greeley.

frequently referred to in the House of Commons, notably by John Bright.

It may also interest readers to know what Marx was paid for his articles—many of them considerably longer even than those here collected. He received £1 for each contribution—not exactly brilliant remuneration.

It will be noted that the twentieth chapter, promised in the nineteenth, does not appear. It may have been written, but was certainly not printed. It was probably crowded out. "I do not know," wrote Mr. Dana, "'how long you intend to make the series, and under ordinary circumstances I should desire to have it prolonged as much as possible. But we have a presidential election at hand, which will occupy our columns to a great extent.... Let me suggest to you if possible to condense your survey ... into say half a dozen more articles" (eleven had then been received by Mr. Dana). "Do not, however, close it without an exposition of the forces now remaining at work there (Germany) and active in the preparation of the future." This "exposition" will be found in the article which I have added to the "Germany" series, on the "Cologne Communist Trial." That trial really gives a complete picture of the conditions of Germany under the triumphant Counter-Revolution.

Marx himself nowhere says the series of letters is incomplete, although he occasionally refers to them. Thus in the letter on the Cologne trial he speaks of the articles, and in 1853 writes: "Those of your readers who, having read my letters on the German Revolution and Counter-Revolution written for the *Tribune* some two years ago, desire to have an immediate intuition of it, will do well to inspect the picture by Mr. Hasenclever now being exhibited in ... New York ... representing the presentation of a workingmen's petition to the magistrates of Düsseldorf in 1848. What the writer could only analyze, the eminent painter has reproduced in its dramatic vitality."

Finally, I would remind English readers that these articles were written when Marx had only been some eighteen months in England, and that he never had any opportunity of reading the proofs. Nevertheless, it has not seemed to me that anything needed correction. I have therefore only removed a few obvious printer's errors.

The date at the head of each chapter refers to the issue of the *Tribune* in which the article appeared, that at the end to the time of writing. I am alone responsible for the headings of the letters as published in this volume.

ELEANOR MARX AVELING.

Sydenham, April, 1896.

CONTENTS

REVOLUTION AND COUNTER - REVOLUTION

I.

GERMANY AT THE OUTBREAK OF THE REVOLUTION.

OCTOBER 25, 1851.

THE first act of the revolutionary drama on the continent of Europe has closed. The "powers that were" before the hurricane of 1848 are again the powers that be," and the more or less popular rulers of a day, provisional governors, triumvirs, dictators, with their tail of representatives, civil commissioners, military commissioners, prefects, judges, generals, officers, and soldiers, are thrown upon foreign shores, and "transported beyond the seas" to England or America, there to form new governments *in partibus infidelium*, European committees, central committees, national committees, and to announce their advent with proclamations quite as solemn as those of any less imaginary potentates.

A more signal defeat than that undergone by
the continental revolutionary party—or rather
parties—upon all points of the line of battle, cannot be imagined. But what of that? Has not
the struggle of the British middle classes for their
social and political supremacy embraced forty-
eight, that of the French middle classes forty
years of unexampled struggles? And was their
triumph ever nearer than at the very moment
when restored monarchy thought itself more
firmly settled than ever? The times of that super-
stition which attributed revolutions to the ill-will
of a few agitators have long passed away. Everyone knows nowadays that wherever there is a revolutionary convulsion, there must be some social
want in the background, which is prevented, by
outworn institutions, from satisfying itself. The
want may not yet be felt as strongly, as generally, as might ensure immediate success: but every
attempt at forcible repression will only bring it
forth stronger and stronger, until it bursts its
fetters. If, then, we have been beaten, we have
nothing else to do but to begin again from the
beginning. And, fortunately, the probably very
short interval of rest which is allowed us between the close of the first and the beginning of
the second act of the movement, gives us time
for a very necessary piece of work: the study of
the causes that necessitated both the late outbreak and its defeat; causes that are not to be
sought for in the accidental efforts, talents,
faults, errors, or treacheries of some of the leaders, but in the general social state and conditions

of existence of each of the convulsed nations. That the sudden movements of February and March, 1848, were not the work of single individuals, but spontaneous, irresistible manifestations of national wants and necessities, more or less clearly understood, but very distinctly felt by numerous classes in every country, is a fact recognized everywhere; but when you inquire into the causes of the counter-revolutionary successes, there you are met on every hand with the ready reply that it was Mr. This or Citizen That who "betrayed" the people. Which reply may be very true or not, according to circumstances, but under no circumstances does it explain anything —not even show how it came to pass that the "people" allowed themselves to be thus betrayed. And what a poor chance stands a political party whose entire stock-in-trade consists in a knowledge of the solitary fact that Citizen So-and-so is not to be trusted.

The inquiry into, and the exposition of, the causes, both of the revolutionary convulsion and its suppression, are, besides, of paramount importance from a historical point of view. All these petty, personal quarrels and recriminations —all these contradictory assertions that it was Marrast, or Ledru Rollin, or Louis Blanc, or any other member of the Provisional Government, or the whole of them, that steered the Revolution amidst the rocks upon which it foundered—of what interest can they be, what light can they afford, to the American or Englishman who observed all these various movements from a distance too great to allow of his distinguishing any of the details of operations? No man in his senses will ever believe that eleven men,* mostly of very indifferent capacity either for good or evil, were able in three months to ruin a nation of thirty-six millions, unless those thirty-six millions saw as little of their way before them as the eleven did. But how it came to pass that thirty-six millions were at once called upon to decide for themselves which way to go, although partly groping in dim twilight, and how then they got lost and their old leaders were for a moment allowed to return to their leadership, that is just the question.

If, then, we try to lay before the readers of *The Tribune* the causes which, while they necessitated the German Revolution of 1848, led quite as inevitably to its momentary repression in 1849 and 1850, we shall not be expected to give a complete history of events as they passed in that country. Later events, and the judgment of coming generations, will decide what portion of that confused mass of seemingly accidental, incoherent, and incongruous facts is to form a part of the world's history. The time for such a task has not yet arrived; we must confine ourselves to the limits of the possible, and be satisfied, if we can find rational causes, based upon undeniable facts, to explain the chief events, the principal vicissitudes of that movement, and to give us a clue as to the direction which the next, and per-

---

*) The "eleven men" were: Dupont de l'Eure, Lamartine, Crémieux, Aarago, Ledru Rollin, Garnier-Pages, Marrast, Clocon, Louis Blanc, and Albert.

haps not very distant, outbreak will impart to the German people.

And firstly, what was the state of Germany at the outbreak of the Revolution?

The composition of the different classes of the people which form the groundwork of every political organization was, in Germany, more complicated than in any other country. While in England and France feudalism was entirely destroyed, or, at least, reduced, as in the former country, to a few insignificant forms, by a powerful and wealthy middle class, concentrated in large towns, and particularly in the capital, the feudal nobility in Germany had retained a great portion of their ancient privileges. The feudal system of tenure was prevalent almost everywhere. The lords of the land had even retained the jurisdiction over their tenants. Deprived of their political privileges, of the right to control the princes, they had preserved almost all their Mediæval supremacy over the peasantry of their demesnes, as well as their exemption from taxes. Feudalism was more flourishing in some localities than in others, but nowhere except on the left bank of the Rhine was it entirely destroyed. This feudal nobility, then extremely numerous and partly very wealthy, was considered, officially, the first "Order" in the country. It furnished the higher Government officials, it almost exclusively officered the army.

The bourgeoisie of Germany was by far not as wealthy and concentrated as that of France or England. The ancient manufactures of Germany had been destroyed by the introduction of steam, and the rapidly extending supremacy of English manufactures; the more modern manufactures, started under the Napoleonic continental system, established in other parts of the country, did not compensate for the loss of the old ones, nor suffice to create a manufacturing interest strong enough to force its wants upon the notice of Governments jealous of every extension of non-noble wealth and power. If France carried her silk manufactures victorious through fifty years of revolutions and wars, Germany, during the same time, all but lost her ancient linen trade.   The manufacturing districts, besides, were few and far between; situated far inland, and using, mostly, foreign, Dutch, or Belgian ports for their imports and exports, they had little or no interest in common with the large seaport towns on the North Sea and the Baltic; they were, above all, unable to create large manufacturing and trading centres, such as Paris and Lyons, London and Manchester. The causes of this backwardness of German manufactures were manifold, but two will suffice to account for it: the unfavorable geographical situation of the country, at a distance from the Atlantic, which had become the great highway for the world's trade, and the continuous wars in which Germany was involved, and which were fought on her soil, from the sixteenth century to the present day. It was this want of numbers, and particularly of anything like concentrated numbers, which prevented the German middle classes from attaining that political supremacy which the English bourgeoisie has enjoyed ever since 1688, and which the French conquered in 1789. And yet, ever since 1815, the wealth, and with the wealth the political importance of the middle class in Germany, was continually growing. Governments were, although reluctantly, compelled to bow, at least to its more immediate material interests. It may even be truly said that from 1815 to 1830, and from 1832 to 1840, every particle of political influence, which, having been allowed to the middle class in the constitutions of the smaller States, was again wrested from them during the above two periods of political reaction, that every such particle was compensated for by some more practical advantage allowed to them. Every political defeat of the middle class drew after it a victory on the field of commercial legislation. And certainly, the Prussian Protective Tariff of 1818, and the formation of the Zollverein, * were worth a good deal more to the traders and manufacturers of Germany than the equivocal right of expressing in the chambers of some diminutive dukedom their want of confidence in ministers who laughed at their votes. Thus, with grow-

---

*) The "Zollverein was the German Customs Union. It was originally founded in 1827, and largely extended after the war of 1866. Since the unification of Germany as an "Empire" in 1871, the States belonging to the Zollverein have been included in the German Empire. The object of the Zollverein was to obtain a uniform rate of customs duties all over Germany.

ing wealth and extending trade, the bourgeoisie soon arrived at a stage where it found the development of its most important interests checked by the political constitution of the country; by its random division among thirty-six princes with conflicting tendencies and caprices; by the feudal fetters upon agriculture and the trade connected with it; by the prying superintendence to which an ignorant and presumptuous bureaucracy subjected all its transactions. At the same time the extension and consolidation of the Zollverein, the general introduction of steam communication, the growing competition in the home trade, brought the commerical classes of the different States and Provinces closer together, equalized their interests and centralized their strength. The natural consequence was the passing of the whole mass of them into the camp of the Liberal Opposition, and the gaining of the first serious struggle of the German middle class for political power. This change may be dated from 1840, from the moment when the bourgeoisie of Prussia assumed the lead of the middle class movement of Germany. We shall hereafter revert to this Liberal Opposition movement of 1840-1847.

The great mass of the nation, which neither belonged to the nobility nor to the bourgeoisie, consisted in the towns of the small trading and shopkeeping class and the working people, and in the country of the peasantry.

The small trading and shopkeeping class is exceedingly numerous in Germany, in consequence

of the stinted development which the large capitalists and manufacturers as a class have had
in that country. In the larger towns it forms
almost the majority of the inhabitants; in the
smaller ones it entirely predominates, from the
absence of wealthier competitors or influence.
This class, a most important one in every modern
body politic, and in all modern revolutions, is still
more important in Germany, where, during the
recent struggles, it generally played the decisive
part. Its intermediate position between the class
of larger capialists, traders, and manufacturers,
the bourgeoisie properly so-called, and the proletarian or industrial class, determines its character. Aspiring to the position of the first, the
least adverse turn of fortune hurls the individuals of this class down into the ranks of the second. In monarchical and feudal countries the
custom of the court and aristocracy becomes necessary to its existence; the loss of this custom
might ruin a great part of it. In the smaller
towns a military garrison, a county government,
a court of law with its followers, form very often
the base of its prosperity; withdraw these, and
down go the shopkeepers, the tailors, the shoe-
makers, the joiners. Thus eternally tossed about
between the hope of entering the ranks of the
wealthier class, and the fear of being reduced
to the state of proletarians or even paupers; between the hope of promoting their interests by
conquering a share in the direction of public affairs, and the dread of rousing, by ill-timed opposition, the ire of a Government which disposes

of their very existence, because it has the power of removing their best customers; possessed of small means, the insecurity of the possession of which is in the inverse ratio of the amount,— this class is extremely vacillating in its views. Humble and crouchingly submissive under a powerful feudal or monarchical Government, it turns to the side of Liberalism when the middle class is in the ascendant; it becomes seized with violent democratic fits as soon as the middle class has secured its own supremacy, but falls back into the abject despondency of fear as soon as the class below itself, the proletarians, attempts an independent movement. We shall by and by see this class, in Germany, pass alternately from one of these stages to the other.

The working class in Germany is, in its social and political development, as far behind that of England and France as the German bourgeoisie is behind the bourgeoisie of those countries. Like master, like man. The evolution of the conditions of existence for a numerous, strong, concentrated, and intelligent proletarian class goes hand in hand with the development of the conditions of existence for a numerous, wealthy, concentrated, and powerful middle class. The working class movement itself never is independent, never is of an exclusively proletarian character until all the different factions of the middle class, and particularly its most progressive faction, the large manufacturers, have conquered political power, and remodelled the State according to their wants. It is then that the inevitable con-

flict beween the employer and the employed becomes imminent, and cannot be adjourned any
longer; that the working class can no longer be
put off with delusive hopes and promises never
to be realized; that the great problem of the nineteenth century, the abolition of the proletariat,
is at last brought forward fairly and in its proper
light. Now, in Germany the mass of the working class were employed, not by those modern
manufacturing lords of which Great Britain fur-
nishes such splendid specimens, but by small
tradesmen, whose entire manufacturing system
is a mere relic of the Middle Ages. And as there
is an enormous difference between the great cot-
ton lord and the petty cobbler cr master tailor,
so there is a corresponding distance from the
wide-awake factory operative of modern manufacturing Babylons to the bashful journeyman
tailor or cabinetmaker of a small country town,
who lives in circumstances and works after a
plan very little different from those of the like
sort of men some five hundred years ago. This
general absence of modern conditions of life, of
modern modes of industrial production, of course
was accompanied by a pretty equally general absence of modern ideas, and it is, therefore, not
to be wondered at if, at the outbreak of the
Revolution, a large part of the working classes
should cry out for the immediate re-establishment of guilds and Mediæval privileged trades'
corporations. Yet from the manufacturing districts, where the modern system of production
predominated, and in consequence of the facil-

ities of inter-communication and mental development afforded by the migratory life of a large number of the working men, a strong nucleus formed itself, whose ideas about the emancipation of their class were far clearer and more in accordance with existing facts and historical necessities; but they were a mere minority. If the active movement of the middle class may be dated from 1840, that of the working class commences its advent by the insurrections of the Silesian and Bohemian factory operatives in 1844, and we shall soon have occasion to pass in review the different stages through which this movement passed.

Lastly, there was the great class of the small farmers, the peasantry, which with its appendix of farm laborers, constitutes a considerable majority of the entire nation. But this class again sub-divided itself into different fractions. There were, firstly, the more wealthy farmers, what is called in Germany *Gross* and *Mittel-Bauern,* proprietors of more or less extensive farms, and each of them commanding the services of several agricultural laborers. This class, placed between the large untaxed feudal landowners, and the smaller peasantry and farm laborers, for obvious reasons found in an alliance with the anti-feudal middle class of the towns its most natural political course. Then there were, secondly, the small freeholders, predominating in the Rhine country, where feudalism had succumbed before the mighty strokes of the great French Revolution. Similar independent small freeholders also

existed here and there in other provinces, where
they had succeeded in buying off the feudal
charges formerly due upon their lands. This
class, however, was a class of freeholders by
name only, their property being generally mort-
gaged to such an extent, and under such onerous
conditions, that not the peasant, but the usurer
who had advanced the money, was the real land-
owner. Thirdly, the feudal tenants, who could
not be easily turned out of their holdings, but who
had to pay a perpetual rent, or to perform in
perpetuity a certain amount of labor in favor
of the lord of the manor. Lastly, the agricultural
laborers, whose condition, in many large farming concerns, was exactly that of the same class
in England, and who in all cases lived and died
poor, ill-fed, and the slaves of their employers.
These three latter classes of the agricultural population, the small freeholders, the feudal tenants, and the agricultural laborers, never troubled their heads much about politics before the
Revolution, but it is evident that this event must
have opened to them a new career, full of brilliant prospects. To every one of them the Revolution offered advantages, and the movement
once fairly engaged in, it was to be expected
that each, in their turn, would join it. But at
the same time it is quite as evident, and equally
borne out by the history of all modern countries,
that the agricultural population, in consequence
of its dispersion over a great space, and of the
difficulty of bringing about an agreement among
any considerable portion of it, never can attempt

a successful independent movement; they require the initiatory impulse of the more concentrated, more enlightened, more easily moved people of the towns.

The preceeding short sketch of the most important of the classes, which in their aggregate formed the German nation at the outbreak of the recent movements, will already be sufficient to explain a great part of the incoherence, incongruence, and apparent contradiction which prevailed in that movement. When interests so varied, so conflicting, so strangely crossing each other, are brought into violent collision; when these contending interests in every district, every province, are mixed in different proportions; when, above all, there is no great centre in the country, no London, no Paris, the decisions of which, by their weight, may supersede the necessity of fighting out the same quarrel over and over again in every single locality; what else is to be expected but that the contest will dissolve itself into a mass of unconnected struggles, in which an enormous quantity of blood, energy, and capital is spent, but which for all that remain without any decisive results?

The political dismemberment of Germany into three dozen of more or less important principalities is equally explained by this confusion and multiplicity of the elements which compose the nation, and which again vary in every locality. Where there are no common interests there can be no unity of purpose, much less of action. The German Confederation, it is true, was declared everlastingly indissoluble; yet the Confederation, and its organ, the Diet, never represented German unity. The very highest pitch to which centralization was ever carried in Germany was the establishment of the Zollverein; by this the States on the North Sea were also forced into a Customs Union of their own, Austria remaining wrapped up in her separate prohibitive tariff. Germany had the satisfaction to be, for all practical purposes divided between three independent powers only, instead of between thirty-six. Of course the paramount supremacy of the Russian Czar, as established in 1814, underwent no change on this account.

Having drawn these preliminary conclusions from our premises, we shall see, in our next, how the aforesaid various classes of the German people were set into movement one after the other, and what character the movement assumed on the outbreak of the French Revolution of 1848.

LONDON, September, 1851.

II.

THE PRUSSIAN STATE.

OCTOBER 28th, 1851.

THE political movement of the middle class
or bourgeoisie, in Germany, may be dated from
1840. It had been preceded by symptoms showing that the moneyed and industrial class of that
country was ripening into a state which would
no longer allow it to continue apathetic and passive under the pressure of a half-feudal, half-
bureaucratic Monarchism. The smaller princes
of Germany, partly to insure to themselves a
greater independence against the supremacy of
Austria and Prussia, or against the influence of
the nobility of their own States, partly in order
to consolidate into a whole the disconnected
provinces united under their rule by the Congress
of Vienna, one after the other granted constitutions of a more or less liberal character. They
could do so without any danger to themselves;
for if the Diet of the Confederation, this mere
puppet of Austria and Prussia, was to encroach
upon their independence as sovereigns, they knew
that in resisting its dictates they would be backed
by public opinion and the Chambers; and if, on
the contrary, these Chambers grew too strong,

they could readily command the power of the Diet to break down all opposition. The Bavarian, Würtemberg, Baden or Hanoverian Constitutional institutions could not, under such circumstances, give rise to any serious struggle for political power, and, therefore, the great bulk of the German middle class kept very generally aloof from the petty squabbles raised in the Legislatures of the small States, well knowing that without a fundamental change in the policy and constitution of the two great powers of Germany, no secondary efforts and victories would be of any avail. But, at the same time, a race of Liberal lawyers, professional oppositionists, sprung up in these small assemblies: the Rottecks, the Welckers, the Roemers, the Jordans, the Stüves, the Eisenmanns, those great "popular men" (*Volksmänner*) who, after a more or less noisy, but always unsuccessful, opposition of twenty years, were carried to the summit of power by the revolutionary springtide of 1848, and who, after having there shown their utter impotency and insignificance, were hurled down again in a moment. These first specimen upon German soil of the trader in politics and opposition, by their speeches and writings made familiar to the German ear the language of Constitutionalism, and by their very existence foreboded the approach of a time when the middle class would seize upon and restore to their proper meaning political phrases which these talkative attorneys and professors were in the habit of using without knowing much about the sense originally attached to them.

German literature, too, labored under the influence of the political excitement into which all Europe had been thrown by the events of 1830. A crude Constitutionalism, or a still cruder Republicanism, were preached by almost all writers of the time. It became more and more the habit, particularly of the inferior sorts of literati, to make up for the want of cleverness in their productions, by political allusions which were sure to attract attention. Poetry, novels, reviews, the drama, every literary production teemed with what was called "tendency," that is with more or less timid exhibitions of an anti-governmental spirit. In order to complete the confusion of ideas reigning after 1830 in Germany, with these elements of political opposition there were mixed up ill-digested university-recollections of German philosophy, and misunderstood gleanings from French Socialism, particularly Saint-Simonism; and the clique of writers who expatiated upon this heterogeneous conglomerate of ideas, presumptuously called themselves "Young Germany," or "the Modern School." They have since repended their youthful sins, but not improved their style of writing.

Lastly, German philosophy, that most complicated, but at the same time most sure thermometer of the development of the German mind, had declared for the middle class, when Hegel in his "Philosophy of Law" pronounced Constitutional Monarchy to be the final and most perfect form of government. In other words, he proclaimed the approaching advent of the middle classes of the country to political power. His school, after his death, did not stop here. While the more advanced section of his followers, on one hand, subjected every religious belief to the ordeal of a rigorous criticism, and shook to its foundation the ancient fabric of Christianity, they at the same time brought forward bolder political principles than hitherto it had been the fate of German ears to hear expounded, and attempted to restore to glory the memory of the heroes of the first French Revolution. The abstruse philosophical language in which these ideas were clothed, if it obscured the mind of both the writer and the reader, equally blinded the eyes of the censor, and thus it was that the "young Hegelian" writers enjoyed a liberty of the Press unknown in every other branch of literature.

Thus it was evident that public opinion was undergoing a great change in Germany. By degrees the vast majority of those classes whose education or position in life enabled them, under an Absolute Monarchy, to gain some political information, and to form anything like an independent political opinion, united into one mighty phalanx of opposition against the existing system. And in passing judgment upon the slowness of political development in Germany no one ought to omit taking into account the difficulty of obtaining correct information upon any subject in a country where all sources of information were under the control of the Government, where from the Ragged School and the Sunday School to the Newspaper and University nothing was said, taught, printed, or published but what had previously obtained its approbation. Look at Vienna, for instance. The people of Vienna, in industry and manufactures, second to none perhaps in Germany; in spirit, courage, and revolutionary energy, proving themselves far superior to all, were yet more ignorant as to their real interests, and committed more blunders during the Revolution than any others, and this was due in a very great measure to the almost absolute ignorance with regard to the very commonest political subjects in which Metternich's Government had succeeded in keeping them.

It needs no further explanation why, under such a system, political information was an almost exclusive monopoly of such classes of society as could afford to pay for its being smuggled into the country, and more particularly of those whose interests were most seriously attacked by the existing state of things, namely, the manufacturing and commercial classes. They, therefore, were the first to unite in a mass against the continuance of a more or less disguised Absolutism, and from their passing into the ranks of the opposition must be dated the beginning of the real revolutionary movement in Germany.

The oppositional pronunciamento of the German bourgeoisie may be dated from 1840, from the death of the late King of Prussia, the last surviving founder of the Holy Alliance of 1815. The new King was known to be no supporter of the predominantly bureaucratic and military monarchy of his father. What the French mid-

dle class had expected from the advent of Louis
XVI., the German bourgeoisie hoped, in some
measure, from Frederick William IV. of Prussia.
It was agreed upon all hands that the old system
was exploded, worn-out, and must be given up;
and what had been borne in silence under the
old King now was loudly proclaimed to be in-
tolerable.

But if Louis XVI., "Louis le Désiré," had been
a plain, unpretending simpleton, half conscious
of his own nullity, without any fixed opinions,
ruled principally by the habits contracted during
his education, "Frederick William le Désiré" was
something quite different. While he certainly
surpassed his French original in weakness of
character, he was neither without pretensions nor
without opinions. He had made himself acquainted, in an amateur sort af way, with the
rudiments of most sciences, and thought himself,
therefore, learned enough to consider final his
judgment upon every subject. He made sure he
was a first-rate orator, and there was certainly
no commercial traveller in Berlin who could beat
him either in prolixity of pretended wit, or in
fluency of elocution. And, above all, he had his
opinions. He hated and despised the bureaucratic
element of the Prussian Monarchy, but only because all his sympathies were with the feudal
element. Himself one of the founders of, and
chief contributors to, the *Berlin Political Weekly
Paper,* the so-called Historical School (a school
living upon the ideas of Bonald, De Maistre, and
other writers of the first generation of French

Legitimists), he aimed at a restoration, as complete as possible, of the predominant social position of the nobility. The King, first nobleman of his realm, surrounded in the first instance by a splendid court of mighty vassals, princes, dukes, and counts; in the second instance, by a numerous and wealthy lower nobility; ruling according to his discretion over his loyal burgesses and peasants, and thus being himself the chief of a complete hierarchy of social ranks or castes, each of which was to enjoy its particular privileges, and to be separated from the others by the almost insurmountable barrier of birth, or of a fixed, inalterable social position; the whole of these castes, or "estates of the realm" balancing each other at the same time so nicely in power and influence that a complete independence of action should remain to the King—such was the *beau idéal* which Frederick William IV. undertook to realize, and which he is again trying to realize at the present moment.

It took some time before the Prussian bourgeoisie, not very well versed in theoretical questions, found out the real purport of their King's tendency. But what they very soon found out was the fact that he was bent upon things quite the reverse of what they wanted. Hardly did the new King find his "gift of the gab" unfettered by his father's death than he set about proclaiming his intentions in speeches without number; and every speech, every act of his, went far to estrange from him the sympathies of the middle class. He would not have cared much for that, if it had not been for some stern and startling realities which interrupted his poetic dreams. Alas, that romanticism is not very quick at accounts, and that feudalism, ever since Don Quixote, reckons without its host! Frederick William IV. partook too much of that contempt of ready cash which ever has been the noblest inheritance of the sons of the Crusaders. He found at his accession a costly, although parsimoniously arranged system of government, and a moderately filled State Treasury. In two years every trace of a surplus was spent in court festivals, royal progresses, largesses, subventions to needy, seedy, and greedy noblemen, etc., and the regular taxes were no longer sufficient for the exigencies of either Court or Government. And thus His Majesty found himself very soon placed between a glaring deficit on one side, and a law of 1820 on the other, by which any new loan, or any increase of the then existing taxation was made illegal without the assent of "the future Representation of the People." This representation did not exist; the new King was less inclined than even his father to create it; and if he had been, he knew that public opinion had wonderfully changed since his accession.

Indeed, the middle classes, who had partly expected that the new King would at once grant a Constitution, proclaim the Liberty of the Press, Trial by Jury, etc., etc.—in short, himself take the lead of that peaceful revolution which they wanted in order to obtain political supremacy— the middle classes had found out their error, and had turned ferociously against the King. In the Rhine Provinces, and more or less generally all over Prussia, they were so exasperated that they, being short themselves of men able to represent them in the Press, went to the length of an alliance with the extreme philosophical party, of which we have spoken above. The fruit of this alliance was the *Rhenish Gazette* of Cologne,* a paper which was suppressed after fifteen months' existence, but from which may be dated the existence of the Newspaper Press in Germany. This was in 1842.

The poor King, whose commercial difficulties were the keenest satire upon his Mediæval propensities, very soon found out that he could not continue to reign without making some slight concession to the popular outcry for that "Representation of the People," which, as the last remnant of the long-forgotten promises of 1813 and 1815, had been embodied in the law of 1820.

---

*) "The Rhenish Gazette." This paper was published at Cologne, as the organ of the Liberal leaders, Hansemann and Camphausen. Marx contributed certain articles on the Landtag, which created so great a sensation that he was offered in 1842—although only 24 years of age—the editorship of the paper. He accepted the offer, and then began his long fight with the Prussian Government. Of course the paper was published under the supervision of a censor, but he, good, easy man, was hopelessly outwitted by the young firebrand. So the Government sent a second "special" censor from Berlin, but the double censorship proved unequal to the task, and in 1843 the paper was suppressed.

He found the least objectionable mode of satisfying this untoward law in calling together the
Standing Committees of the Provincial Diets.
The Provincial Diets had been instituted in 1823.
They consisted for every one of the eight provinces of the kingdom :—(1) Of the higher nobility, the formerly sovereign families of the German Empire, the heads of which were members
of the Diet by birthright. (2) Of the representatives of the knights, or lower nobility. (3) Of
representatives of towns. (4) Of deputies of the
peasantry, or small farming class. The whole
was arranged in such a manner that in every
province the two sections of the nobility always
had a majority of the Diet. Every one of these
eight Provincial Diets elected a Committee, and
these eight Committees were now called to Berlin in order to form a Representative Assembly
for the purpose of voting the much-desired loan.
It was stated that the Treasury was full, and that
the loan was required, not for current wants, but
for the construction of a State railway. But the
united Committees gave the King a flat refusal,
declaring themselves incompetent to act as the
representatives of the people, and called upon
His Majesty to fulfil the promise of a Representative Constitution which his father had given,
when he wanted the aid of the people against
Napoleon.

The sitting of the united Committees proved
that the spirit of opposition was no longer confined to the bourgeoisie. A part of the peasantry
had joined them, and many nobles, being them-

selves large farmers on their own properties, and dealers in corn, wool, spirits, and flax, requiring the same guarantees against absolutism, bureaucracy, and feudal restoration, had equally pronounced against the Government, and for a Representative Constitution. The King's plan had signally failed; he had got no money, and had increased the power of the opposition. The subsequent sitting of the Provincial Diets themselves was still more unfortunate for the King. All of them asked for reforms, for the fulfilment of the promises of 1813 and 1815, for a Constitution and a Free Press; the resolutions to this effect of some of them were rather disrespectfully worded, and the ill-humored replies of the exasperated King made the evil still greater.

In the meantime, the financial difficulties of the Government went on increasing. For a time, abatements made upon the moneys appropriated for the different public services, fraudulent transactions with the "Seehandlung," a commercial establishment speculating and trading for account and risk of the State, and long since acting as its money-broker, had sufficed to keep up appearances; increased issues of State paper-money had furnished some resources; and the secret, upon the whole, had been pretty well kept. But all these contrivances were soon exhausted. There was another plan tried: the establishment of a bank, the capital of which was to be furnished partly by the State and partly by private shareholders; the chief direction to belong to the State, in such a manner as to enable the Government to draw upon the funds of this bank to a large amount, and thus to repeat the same fraudulent transactions that would no longer do with the "Seehandlung." But, as a matter of course, there were no capitalists to be found who would hand over their money upon such conditions; the statutes of the bank had to be altered, and the property of the shareholders guaranteed from the encroachments of the Treasury, before any shares were subscribed for. Thus, this plan having failed, there remained nothing but to try a loan, if capitalists could be found who would lend their cash without requiring the permission and guarantee of that mysterious "future Representation of the People." Rothchild was applied to, and he declared that if the loan was to be guaranteed by this "Representation of the People," he would undertake the thing at a moment's notice —if not, he could not have anything to do with the transaction.

Thus every hope of obtaining money had vanished, and there was no possibility of escaping the fatal "Representation of the People." Rothschild's refusal was known in autumn, 1846, and in February of the next year the King called together all the eight Provincial Diets to Berlin, forming them into one "United Diet." This Diet was to do the work required, in case of need, by the law of 1820; it was to vote loans and increased taxes, but beyond that it was to have no rights. Its voice upon general legislation was to be merely consultative; it was to assemble, not at fixed periods, but whenever it pleased the King;

it was to discuss nothing but what the Government pleased to lay before it. Of course, the members were very little satisfied with the part they were expected to perform. They repeated the wishes they had enounced when they met in the provincial assembles; the relations between them and the Government soon became acrimonious, and when the loan, which was again stated to be required for railway constructions, was demanded from them, they again refused to grant it.

This vote very soon brought their sitting to a close. The King, more and more exasperated, dismissed them with a reprimand, but still remained without money. And, indeed, he had every reason to be alarmed at his position, seeing that the Liberal League, headed by the middle classes, comprising a large part of the lower nobility, and all the different sections of the lower orders—that this Liberal League was determined to have what it wanted. In vain the King had declared, in the opening speech, that he would never, never grant a Constitution in the modern sense of the word; the Liberal League insisted upon such a modern, anti-feudal, Representative Constitution, with all its sequels, Liberty of the Press, Trial by Jury, etc.; and before they got it, not a farthing of money would they grant. There was one thing evident: that things could not go on long in this manner, and that either one of the parties must give way, or that a rupture—a bloody struggle—must ensue. And the middle classes knew that they were on the eve of a revolution, and they prepared themselves for it. They sought to obtain by every possible means the support of the working class of the towns, and of the peasantry in the agricultural districts, and it is well known that there was, in the latter end of 1847, hardly a single prominent political character among the bourgeoisie who did not proclaim himself a "Socialist," in order to insure to himself the sympathy of the proletarian class. We shall see these "Socialists" at work by and by.

This eagerness of the leading bourgeoisie to adopt, at least the outward show of Socialism, was caused by a great change that had come over the working classes of Germany. There had been ever since 1840 a fraction of German workmen, who, travelling in France and Switzerland, had more or less imbibed the crude Socialist or Communist notions then current among the French workmen. The increasing attention paid to similar ideas in France ever since 1840 made Socialism and Communism fashionable in Germany also, and as far back as 1843, all newspapers teemed with discussions of social questions. A school of Socialists very soon formed itself in Germany, distinguished more for the obscurity than for the novelty of its ideas; its principal efforts consisted in the translation of French Fourierist, Saint-Simonian, and other doctrines into the abstruse language of German philosophy. The German Communist school, entirely different from this sect, was formed about the same time.

In 1844, there occurred the Silesian weavers'

riots, followed by the insurrection of the calico printers of Prague. These riots, cruelly suppressed, riots of working men not against the Government, but against their employers, created a deep sensation, and gave a new stimulus to Socialist and Communist propaganda amongst the working people. So did the bread riots during the year of famine, 1847. In short, in the same manner as Constitutional Opposition rallied around its banner the great bulk of the propertied classes (with the exception of the large feudal land-holders), so the working classes of the larger towns looked for their emancipation to the Socialist and Communist doctrines, although, under the then existing Press laws, they could be made to know only very little about them. They could not be expected to have any very definite ideas as to what they wanted; they only knew that the programme of the Constitutional bourgeoisie did not contain all they wanted, and that their wants were no wise contained in the Constitutional circle of ideas.

There was then no separate Republican party in Germany. People were either Constitutional Monarchists, or more or less clearly defined Socialists or Communists.

With such elements the slightest collision must have brought about a great revolution. While the higher nobility and the older civil and military officers were the only safe supports of the existing system; while the lower nobility, the trading middle classes, the universities, the school-masters of every degree, and even part of the lower ranks of the bureaucracy and military officers were all leagued against the Goverment; while behind these there stood the dissatisfied masses of the peasantry, and of the proletarians of the large towns, supporting, for the time being, the Liberal Opposition, but already muttering strange words about taking things into their own hands; while the bourgeoisie was ready to hurl down the Government, and the proletarians were preparing to hurl down the bourgeoisie in its turn; this Government went on obstinately in a course which must bring about a collision. Germany was, in the beginning of 1848, on the eve of a revolution, and this revolution was sure to come, even had the French Revolution of February not hastened it.

What the effects of this Parisian Revolution were upon Germany we shall see in our next.

LONDON, September, 1851.

III.

THE OTHER GERMAN STATES.

In our last we confined ourselves almost exclusively to that State which, during the years 1840 to 1848, was by far the most important in the German movement, namely, to Prussia. It is, however, time to pass a rapid glance over the other States of Germany during the same period.

As to the petty States, they had, ever since the revolutionary movements of 1830, completely passed under the dictatorship of the Diet, that is of Austria and Prussia. The several Constitutions, established as much as a means of defence against the dictates of the larger States, as to insure popularity to their princely authors, and unity to heterogeneous Assemblies of Provinces, formed by the Congress of Vienna, without any leading principle whatever—these Constitutions, illusory as they were, had yet proved dangerous to the authority of the petty princes themselves during the exciting times of 1830 and 1831. They were all but destroyed; whatever of them was allowed to remain was less than a shadow, and it required the loquacious self-complacency of a

44

Welcker, a Rotteck, a Dahlmann, to imagine that any results could possibly flow from the humble opposition, mingled with degrading flattery, which they were allowed to show off in the impotent Chambers of these petty States.

The more energetic portion of the middle class in these smaller States, very soon after 1840, abandoned all the hopes they had formerly based upon the development of Parliamentary government in these dependencies of Austria and Prussia. No sooner had the Prussian bourgeoisie and the classes allied to it shown a serious resolution to struggle for Parliamentary government in Prussia, than they were allowed to take the lead of the Constitutional movement over all non-Austrian Germany. It is a fact which now will not any longer be contested, that the nucleus of those Constitutionalists of Central Germany, who afterwards seceded from the Frankfort National Assembly, and who, from the place of their separate meetings, were called the Gotha party, long before 1848 contemplated a plan which, with little modification, they in 1849 proposed to the representatives of all Germany. They intended a complete exclusion of Austria from the German Confederation, the establishment of a new Confederation, with a new fundamental law, and with a Federal Parliament, of the more insignificant States into the larger ones. All this was to be carried out the moment Prussia entered into the ranks of Constitutional Monarchy, established the Liberty of the Press, assumed a policy independent from that of Russia and Austria, and thus enabled the Constitutionalists of the lesser States to obtain a real control over their respective Governments. The inventor of this scheme was Professor Gervinus, of Heidelberg (Baden). Thus the emancipation of the Prussian bourgeoisie was to be the signal for that of the middle classes of Germany generally, and for an alliance, offensive and defensive of both against Russia and Austria, for Austria was, as we shall see presently, considered as an entirely barbarian country, of which very little was known, and that little not to the credit of its population; Austria, therefore, was not considered as an essential part of Germany.

As to the other classes of society, in the smaller States they followed, more or less rapidly, in the wake of their equals in Prussia. The shopkeeping class got more and more dissatisfied with their respective Governments, with the increase of taxation, with the curtailments of those political sham-privileges of which they used to boast when comparing themselves to the "slaves of despotism" in Austria and Prussia; but as yet they had nothing definite in their opposition which might stamp them as an independent party, distinct from the Constitutionalism of the higher bourgeoisie. The dissatisfaction among the peasantry was equally growing, but it is well known that this section of the people, in quiet and peaceful times, will never assert its interests and assume its position as an independent class, except in countries where universal suffrage is established. The working classes in the trades and manufactures of the towns commenced to be infected with the "poison" of Socialism and Communism, but there being few towns of any importance out of Prussia, and still fewer manufacturing districts, the movement of this class, owing to the want of centres of action and propaganda, was extremely slow in the smaller States.

Both in Prussia and in the smaller States the difficulty of giving vent to political opposition created a sort of religious opposition in the parallel movements of German Catholicism and Free Congregationalism. History affords us numerous examples where, in countries which enjoy the blessings of a State Church, and where political discussion is fettered, the profane and dangerous opposition against the worldly power is hid under the more sanctified and apparently more disinterested struggle against spiritual despotism. Many a Government that will not allow of any of its acts being discussed, will hesitate before it creates martyrs and excites the religious fanaticism of the masses. Thus in Germany, in 1845, in every State, either the Roman Catholic or the Protestant religion, or both, were considered part and parcel of the law of the land. In every State, too, the clergy of either of those denominations, or of both, formed an essential part of the bureaucratic establishment of the Government. To attack Protestant or Catholic orthodoxy, to attack priestcraft, was then to make an underhand attack upon the Government itself. As to the German Catholics, their very existence was an attack upon the Catholic Governments of Germany, particularly Austria and Bavaria; and as such it was taken by those Governments. The Free Congregationalists, Protestant Dissenters, somewhat resembling the English and American Unitarians, openly professed their opposition to the clerical and rigidly orthodox tendency of the King of Prussia and his favourite Minister for the Educational and Clerical Department, Mr. Eickhorn. The two new sects, rapidly extending for a moment, the first in Catholic, the second in Protestant countries, had no other distinction but their different origin; as to their tenets, they perfectly agreed upon this most important point — that all definite dogmas were nugatory. This want of any definition was their very essence; they pretended to build that great temple under the roof of which all Germans might unite; they thus represented, in a religious form, another political idea of the day—that of German unity, and yet they could never agree among themselves.

The idea of German unity, which the abovementioned sects sought to realize, at least, upon religious ground, by inventing a common religion for all Germans, manufactured expressly for their use, habits, and taste—this idea was, indeed, very widely spread, particularly in the smaller States. Ever since the dissolution of the German Empire by Napoleon, the cry for a union of all the *disjecta membra* of the German body had been the most general expression of discontent with the established order of things, and

most so in the smaller States, where costliness
of a court, an administration, an army, in short,
the dead weight of taxation, increased in a direct
ratio with the smallness and impotency of the
State. But what this German unity was to be
when carried out was a question upon which
parties disagreed. The bourgeoisie, which wanted
no serious revolutionary convulsion, were satisfied with what we have seen they considered
"practicable," namely a union of all Germany,
exclusive of Austria, under the supremacy of a
Constitutional Government of Prussia; and surely, without conjuring dangerous storms, nothing
more could, at that time, be done. The shopkeeping class and the peasantry, as far as these latter troubled themselves about such things, never
arrived at any definition of that German unity
they so louldly clamoured after; a few dreamers,
mostly feudalist reactionists, hoped for the re-
establishment of the German Empire; some few
ignorant, *soi-disant* Radicals, admiring Swiss institutions, of which they had not yet made that
practical experience which afterwards most ludi-
crously undeceived them, pronounced for a Fed-
erated Republic; and it was only the most extreme party which, at that time, dared pronounce
for a German Republic, one and indivisible.
Thus, German unity was in itself a question big
with disunion, discord, and, in the case of certain eventualities, even civil war.

To resume, then; this was the state of Prussia,
and the smaller States of Germany, at the end
of 1847. The middle class, feeling their power,

and resolved not to endure much longer the fetters with which a feudal and bureaucratic despotism enchained their commercial transactions, their industrial productivity, their common action as a class; a portion of the landed nobility so far changed into producers of mere marketable commodities, as to have the same interests and to make common cause with the middle class; the smaller trading class, dissatisfied, grumbling at the taxes, at the impediments thrown in the way of their business, but without any definite plan for such reforms as should secure their position in the social and political body; the peasantry, oppressed here by feudal exactions, there by money-lenders, usurers, and lawyers; the working people of the towns infected with the general discontent, equally hating the Government and the large industrial capitalists, and catching the contagion of Socialist and Communist ideas; in short, a heterogeneous mass of opposition, springing from various interests, but more or less led on by the bourgeoisie, in the first ranks of which again marched the bourgeoisie of Prussia, and particularly of the Rhine Province. On the other hand, Governments disagreeing upon many points, distrustful of each other, and particularly of that of Prussia, upon which yet they had to rely for protection; in Prussia a Government forsaken by public opinion, forsaken by even a portion of the nobility, leaning upon an army and a bureaucracy which every day got more infected by the ideas, and subjected to the influence, of the oppositional bourgeoisie—a Government, besides all this, penniless in the most literal meaning of the word, and which could not procure a single cent to cover its increasing deficit, but by surrendering at discretion to the opposition of the bourgeoisie. Was there ever a more splendid position for the middle class of any country, while it struggled for power against the established Government?

LONDON, September, 1851.

IV.

AUSTRIA.

November 7th, 1851.

We have now to consider Austria; that country which, up to March, 1848, was sealed up to the eyes of foreign nations almost as much as China before the late war with England.

As a matter of course, we can here take into consideration nothing but German Austria. The affairs of the Polish, Hungarian, or Italian Austrians do not belong to our subject, and as far as they, since 1848, have influenced the fate of the German Austrians, they will have to be taken into account hereafter.

The Government of Prince Metternich turned upon two hinges; firstly, to keep every one of the different nations subjected to the Austrian rule, in check, by all other nations similarly conditioned; secondly, and this always has been the fundamental principle of absolute monarchies, to rely for support upon two classes, the feudal landlords and the large stockjobbing capitalists; and to balance, at the same time, the influence and power of either of these classes by that of the other, so as to leave full independ-

ence of action to the Government. The landed
nobility, whose entire income consisted in feudal
revenues of all sorts, could not but support a
Government which proved their only protection
against that down-trodden class of serfs upon
whose spoils they lived; and whenever the less
wealthy portion of them, as in Galicia, in 1846,
rose in opposition against the Government, Metternich in an instant let loose upon them these
very serfs, who at any rate profited by the occasion to wreak a terrible vengeance upon their
more immediate oppressors. On the other hand,
the large capitalists of the Exchange were
chained to Metternich's Government by the vast
share they had in the public funds of the country. Austria, restored to her full power in 1815
restoring and maintaining in Italy Absolute Monarchy ever since 1820, freed from part of her
liabilities by the bankruptcy of 1810, had, after
the peace, very soon re-established her credit in
the great European money markets; and in pro-
portion as her credit grew, she had drawn
against it. Thus all the large European money-
dealers had engaged considerable portions of
their capital in the Austrian funds; they all of
them were interested in upholding the credit of
that country, and as Austrian public credit, in
order to be upheld, ever required new loans, they
were obliged from time to time to advance new
capital in order to keep up the credit of the secur-
ities for that which they already had advanced.
The long peace after 1815, and the apparent impossibility of a thousand years old empire, like

Austria, being upset, increased the credit of Metternich's Government in a wonderful ratio, and made it even independent of the good will of the Vienna bankers and stock-jobbers; for as long as Metternich could obtain plenty of money at Frankfort and Amsterdam, he had, of course, the satisfaction of seeing the Austrian capitalists at his feet. They were, besides, in every other respect at his mercy; the large profits which bankers, stock-jobbers, and Government contractors always contrive to draw out of an absolute monarchy, were compensated for by the almost unlimited power which the Government possessed over their persons and fortunes; and not the smallest shadow of an opposition was, therefore, to be expected from this quarter. Thus Metternich was sure of the support of the two most powerful and influential classes of the empire, and he possessed besides an army and a bureaucracy, which for all purposes of absolutism could not be better constituted. The civil and military officers in the Austrian service form a race of their own; their fathers have been in the service of the Kaiser, and so will their sons be; they belong to none of the multifarious nationalities congregated under the wing of the double-headed eagle; they are, and ever have been, removed from one end of the empire to the other, from Poland to Italy, from Germany to Transylvania; Hungarian, Pole, German, Roumanian, Italian, Croat, every individual not stamped with "imperial and royal authority," etc., bearing a separate national character, is equally despised by them; they have no nationality, or rather, they alone make up the really Austrian nation. It is evident what a pliable, and at the same time powerful instrument, in the hands of an intelligent and energetic chief, such a civil and military hierarchy must be.

As to the other classes of the population, Metternich, in the true spirit of a statesman of the *ancien régime,* cared little for their support. He had, with regard to them, but one policy: to draw as much as possible out of them in the shape of taxation, and at the same time, to keep them quiet. The trading and manufacturing middle class was but of slow growth in Austria. The trade of the Danube was comparatively unimportant; the country possessed but one port, Trieste, and the trade of the port was very limited. As to the manufacturers, they enjoyed considerable protection, amounting even in most cases to the complete exclusion of all foreign competition; but this advantage had been granted to them principally with a view to increase their tax-paying capabilities, and was in a high degree counterpoised by internal restrictions on manufactures, privileges on guilds, and other feudal corporations, which were scrupulously upheld as long as they did not impede the purposes and views of the Government. The petty tradesmen were encased in the narrow bounds of these Mediæval guilds, which kept the different trades in a perpetual war of privilege against each other, and at the same time, by all but excluding individuals of the working class from the possibility

of raising themselves in the social scale, gave a
sort of hereditary stability to the members of
those involuntary associations. Lastly, the peasant and the working man were treated as mere
taxable matter, and the only care that was taken
of them was to keep them as much as possible
in the same conditions of life in which they then
existed, and in which their fathers had existed
before them. For this purpose every old, established, hereditary authority was upheld in the
same manner as that of the State; the authority
of the landlord over the petty tenant farmer, that
of the manufacturer over the operative, of the
small master over the journeyman and apprent-
ice, of the father over the son, was everywhere
rigidly maintained by the Government, and every
branch of disobedience punished the same as a
transgression of the law, by that universal instrument of Austrian justice—the stick.

Finally, to wind up into one comprehensive
system all these attempts at creating an artificial
stability, the intellectual food allowed to the nation was selected with the minutest caution, and
dealt out as sparingly as possible. Education
was everywhere in the hands of the Catholic
priesthood, whose chiefs, in the same manner as
the large feudal landowners, were deeply interested in the conservation of the existing system.
The universities were organized in a manner
which allowed them to produce nothing but special men, that might or might not obtain great
proficiency in sundry particular branches of
knowledge, but which, at all events, excluded

that universal liberal education which other universities are expected to impart. There was absolutely no newspaper press, except in Hungary, and the Hungarian papers were prohibited in all other parts of the monarchy. As to general literature, its range had not widened for a century; it had narrowed again after the death of Joseph II. And all around the frontier, whereever the Austrian States touched upon a civilized country, a cordon of literary censors was established in connection with the cordon of customhouse officials, preventing any foreign book or newspaper from passing into Austria before its contents had been twice or three times thoroughly sifted, and found pure of even the slightest contamination of the malignant spirit of the age.

For about thirty years after 1815 this system worked with wonderful success. Austria remained almost unknown to Europe, and Europe was quite as little known in Austria. The social state of every class of the population, and of the population as a whole, appeared not to have undergone the slightest change. Whatever rancour there might exist from class to class—and the existence of this rancour was for Metternich a principal condition of government, which he even fostered by making the higher classes the instruments of all Government exactions, and thus throwing the odium upon them—whatever hatred the people might bear to the inferior officials of the State, there existed, upon the whole, little or no dissatisfaction with the Central Government. The Emperor was adored, and old Francis I.

seemed to be borne out by facts when, doubting of the durability of this system, he complacently added: "And yet it will hold while I live, and Metternich."

But there was a slow underground movement going on which baffled all Metternich's efforts. The wealth and influence of the manufacturing and trading middle class increased. The introduction of machinery and steam-power in manufactures upset in Austria, as it had done everywhere else, the old relations and vital conditions of whole classes of society; it changed serfs into free men, small farmers into manufacturing operatives; it undermined the old feudal trades-corporations, and destroyed the means of existence of many of them. The new commercial and manufacturing population came everywhere into collision with the old feudal institutions. The middle classes, more and more induced by their business to travel abroad, introduced some mythical knowledge of the civilized countries situated beyond the Imperial line of customs; the introduction of railways finally accelerated both the industrial and intellectual movement. There was, too, a dangerous part in the Austrian State establishment, *viz.*, the Hungarian feudal Constitution, with its parliamentary proceedings, and its struggles of the impoverished and oppositional mass of the nobility against the Government and its allies, the magnates. Presburg, the seat of the Diet, was at the very gates of Vienna. All the elements contributed to create among the middle classes of the towns a spirit, not exactly of opposition, for opposition was as yet impossible, but of discontent; a general wish for reforms, more of an administrative than of a constitutional nature. And in the same manner as in Prussia, a portion of the bureaucracy joined the bourgeoisie. Among this hereditary caste of officials the traditions of Joseph II. were not forgotten; the more educated functionaries of the Government, who themselves sometimes meddled with imaginary possible reforms, by far preferred the progressive and intellectual despotism of that Emperor to the "paternal" despotism of Metternich. A portion of the poorer nobility equally sided with the middle class, and as to the lower classes of the population, who always had found plenty of grounds to complain of their superiors, if not of the Government, they in most cases could not but adhere to the reformatory wishes of the bourgeoisie.

It was about this time, say 1843 or 1844, that a particular branch of literature, agreeable to this change, was established in Germany. A few Austrian writers, novelists, literary critics, bad poets, the whole of them of very indifferent ability, but gifted with that peculiar industrialism proper to the Jewish race, established themselves in Leipsic and other German towns out of Austria, and there, out of the reach of Metternich, published a number of books and pamphlets on Austrian affairs. They and their publishers made "a roaring trade" of it. All Germany was eager to become initiated into the secrets of the policy of European China; and the Austrians themselves, who obtained these publications by the wholesale smuggling carried on upon the Bohemian frontier, were still more curious. Of course, the secrets let out in these publications were of no great importance, and the reform plans schemed out by their well-wishing authors bore the stamp of an innocuousness almost amounting to political virginity. A Constitution and a free press for Austria were things considered unattainable; administrative reforms, extension of the rights of the Provincial Diets, admission of foreign books and newspapers, and a less severe censorship—the loyal and humble desires of these good Austrians did hardly go any farther.

At all events the growing impossibility of preventing the literary intercourse of Austria with the rest of Germany, and through Germany with the rest of the world, contributed much toward the formation of an anti-Governmental public opinion, and brought at least some little political information within the reach of part of the Austrian population. Thus, by the end of 1847, Austria was seized, although in an inferior degree, by that political and politico-religious agitation which then prevailed in all Germany; and if its progress in Austria was more silent, it did, nevertheless, find revolutionary elements enough to work upon. There was the peasant, serf, or feudal tenant, ground down into the dust by lordly or Government exactions; then the factory operative, forced by the stick of the policeman to work upon any terms the manufacturer chose to grant; then the journeyman, debarred by the corporative laws from any chance of gaining an independence in his trade; then the merchant, stumbling at every step in business over absurd regulations; then the manufacturer, in uninterrupted conflict with trade-guilds, jealous of their privileges, or with greedy and meddling officials; then the school-master, the *savant*, the better educated functionary, vainly struggling against an ignorant and presumptuous clergy, or a stupid and dictating superior. In short, there was not a single class satisfied, for the small concessions Government was obliged now and then to make were not made at its own expense, for the treasury could not afford that, but at the expense of the high aristocracy and clergy; and as to the great bankers, and fundholders, the late events in Italy, the increasing opposition of the Hungarian Diet, and the unwonted spirit of discontent and cry for reform, manifesting themselves all over the Empire, were not of a nature to strengthen their faith in the solidity and solvency of the Austrian Empire.

Thus Austria, too, was marching slowly but surely toward a mighty change, when, of a sudden, an event broke out in France, which at once brought down the impending storm, and gave the lie to old Francis's assertion, that the building would hold out both during his and Metternich's lifetime.

LONDON, September, 1851.

V.

THE VIENNA INSURRECTION.

November 12, 1851.

On the 24th of February, 1848, Louis Philippe was driven out of Paris, and the French Republic was proclaimed. On the 13th of March following, the people of Vienna broke the power of Prince Metternich, and made him flee shamefully out of the country. On the 18th of March the people of Berlin rose in arms, and, after an obstinate struggle of eighteen hours, had the satisfaction of seeing the King surrender himself into their hands. Simultaneous outbreaks of a more or less violent nature, but all with the same success, occurred in the capitals of the smaller States of Germany. The German people, if they had not accomplished their first revolution, were at least fairly launched into the revolutionary career.

As to the incidents of these various insurrections, we cannot enter here into the details of them: what we have to explain is their character, and the position which the different classes of the population took up with regard to them.

The Revolution of Vienna may be said to have

been made by an almost unanimous population.
The bourgeoisie (with the exception of the bankers and stock-jobbers), the petty trading class,
the working people, one and all arose at once
against a Government detested by all, a Government so universally hated, that the small minority of nobles and money lords which had supported it made itself invisible on the very first
attack. The middle classes had been kept in such
a degree of political ignorance by Metternich
that to them the news from Paris about the reign
of Anarchy, Socialism, and terror, and about impending struggles between the class of capitalists and the class of laborers, proved quite unintelligible. They, in their political innocence,
either could attach no meaning to these news,
or they believed them to be fiendish inventions of
Metternich, to frighten them into obedience.
They, besides, had never seen working men acting as a class, or stand up for their own distinct
class interests. They had, from their past experience, no idea of the possibility of any differences
springing up between classes that now were so
heartily united in upsetting a Government hated
by all.   They saw the working people agree with
themselves upon all points: a Constitution, Trial
by Jury, Liberty of the Press, etc. Thus they
were, in March, 1848, at least, heart and soul
with the movement, and the movement, on the
other hand, at once constituted them the (at
least in theory) predominant class of the State.
    But it is the fate of all revolutions that this
union of different classes, which in some degree

is always the necessary condition of any revolution, cannot subsist long. No sooner is the victory gained against the common enemy than the victors become divided among themselves into different camps, and turn their weapons against each other. It is this rapid and passionate development of class antagonism which, in old and complicated social organisms, makes a revolution such a powerful agent of social and political progress; it is this incessantly quick upshooting of new parties succeeding each other in power, which, during those violent commotions, makes a nation pass in five years over more ground than it would have done in a century under ordinary circumstances.

The Revolution in Vienna made the middle class the theoretically predominant class; that is to say, the concessions wrung from the Government were such as, once carried out practically and adhered to for a time, would inevitably have secured the supremacy of the middle class. But practically the supremacy of that class was far from being established. It is true that by the establishment of a national guard, which gave arms to the bourgeoisie and petty tradesmen, that class obtained both force and importance; it is true that by the installation of a "Committee of Safety," a sort of revolutionary, irresponsible Government in which the bourgeoisie predominated, it was placed at the head of power. But, at the same time, the working classes were partially armed too; they and the students had borne the brunt of the fight, as far as fight there had

been; and the students, about 4,000 strong, well-
armed, and far better disciplined than the national guard, formed the nucleus, the real
strength of the revolutionary force, and were no
ways willing to act as a mere instrument in the
hands of the Committee of Safety. Though they
recognized it, and were even its most enthusiastic
supporters, they yet formed a sort of independent and rather turbulent body, deliberating for
themselves in the "Aula," keeping an intermediate position between the bourgeoisie and the
working-classes, preventing by constant agitation things from settling down to the old every-
day tranquillity, and very often forcing their
resolutions upon the Committee of Safety. The
working men, on the other hand, almost entirely thrown out of employment, had to be
employed in public works at the expense of the
State, and the money for this purpose had, of
course, to be taken out of the purse of the tax-
payers or out of the chest of the city of Vienna.
All this could not but become very unpleasant
to the tradesmen of Vienna. The manufactures
of the city, calculated for the consumption of the
rich and aristocratic courts of a large country,
were as a matter of course entirely stopped by
the Revolution, by the flight of the aristocracy
and Court; trade was at a standstill, and the continuous agitation and excitement kept up by the
students and working people was certainly not
the means to "restore confidence," as the phrase
went. Thus a certain coolness very soon sprung
up between the middle classes on the one side

and the turbulent students and working people on the other; and if for a long time this coolness was not ripened into open hostility, it was because the Ministry, and particularly the Court, in their impatience to restore the old order of things, constantly justified the suspicions and the turbulent activity of the more revolutionary parties, and constantly made arise, even before the eyes of the middle classes, the spectre of old Metternichian despotism.   Thus on the 15th of May, and again on the 16th, there were fresh risings of all classes in Vienna, on account of the Government having tried to attack, or to undermine some of the newly-conquered liberties, and on each occasion the alliance between the national guard or armed middle class, the students, and the workingmen, was again cemented for a time.

As to the other classes of the population, the aristocracy and the money lords had disappeared, and the peasantry were busily engaged everywhere in removing, down to the very last vestiges of feudalism.   Thanks to the war in Italy, and the occupation which Vienna and Hungary gave to the Court, they were left at full liberty, and succeeded in their work of liberation, in Austria, better than in any other part of Germany. The Austrian Diet had very shortly after only to confirm the steps already practically taken by the peasantry, and whatever else the Government of Prince Schwartzenberg may be enabled to restore, it will never have the power of re-establishing the feudal servitude of the peasantry.   And if Austria at the present moment is again comparatively tranquil, and even strong, it is principally because the great majority of the people, the peasants, have been real gainers by the Revolution, and because whatever else has been attacked by the restored Government, those palpable, substantial advantages, conquered by the peasantry, are as yet untouched.

LONDON, October, 1851.

VI.

THE BERLIN INSURRECTION

NOVEMBER 28, 1851.

THE second center of revolutionary action was Berlin, and from what has been stated in the foregoing papers, it may be guessed that there this action was far from having that unanimous support of almost all classes by which it was accompanied in Vienna. In Prussia, the bourgeoisie had been already involved in actual struggles with the Government; a rupture had been the result of the "United Diet"; a bourgeois revolution was impending, and that revolution might have been, in its first outbreak, quite as unanimous as that of Vienna, had it not been for the Paris Revolution of February. That event precipitated everything, while at the same time it was carried out under a banner totally different from that under which the Prussian bourgeoisie was preparing to defy its Government. The Revolution of February upset, in France, the very same sort of Government which the Prussian bourgeoisie were going to set up in their own country. The Revolution of February announced

68

itself as a revolution of the working classes against the middle classes; it proclaimed the downfall of middle-class government and the emancipation of the workingman. Now the Prussian bourgeoisie had, of late, had quite enough of working-class agitation in their own country. After the first terror of the Silesian riots had passed away, they had even tried to give this agitation a turn in their own favor; but they always had retained a salutary horror of revolutionary Socialism and Communism; and, therefore, when they saw men at the head of the Government in Paris whom they considered as the most dangerous enemies of property, order, religion, family, and of the other *Penates* of the modern bourgeois, they at once experienced a considerable cooling down of their own revolutionary ardor. They knew that the moment must be seized, and that, without the aid of the working masses, they would be defeated; and yet their courage failed them. Thus they sided with the Government in the first partial and provincial outbreaks, tried to keep the people quiet in Berlin, who, during five days, met in crowds before the royal palace to discuss the news and ask for changes in the Government; and when at last, after the news of the downfall of Metternich, the King made some slight concessions, the bourgeoisie considered the Revolution as completed, and went to thank His Majesty for having fulfilled all the wishes of his people. But then followed the attack of the military on the crowd, the barricades, the struggle, and the defeat of royalty. Then everything was changed; the very working classes, which it had been the tendency of the bourgeoisie to keep in the background, had been pushed forward, had fought and conquered, and all at once were conscious of their strength. Restrictions of suffrage, of the liberty of the press, of the right to sit on juries, of the right of meeting—restrictions that would have been very agreeable to the bourgeoisie because they would have touched upon such classes only as were beneath them — now were no longer possible. The danger of a repetition of the Parisian scenes of "anarchy" was imminent. Before this danger all former differences disappeared. Against the victorious workingman, although he had not yet uttered any specific demands for himself, the friends and the foes of many years united, and the alliance between the bourgeoisie and the supporters of the over-turned system was concluded upon the very barricades of Berlin. The necessary concessions, but no more than was unavoidable, were to be made, a ministry of the opposition leaders of the United Diet was to be formed, and in return for its services in saving the Crown, it was to have the support of all the props of the old Government, the feudal aristocracy, the bureaucracy, the army. These were the conditions upon which Messrs. Camphausen and Hansemann undertook the formation of a cabinet.

Such was the dread evinced by the new ministers of the aroused masses, that in their eyes every means was good if it only tended to strenghthen the shaken foundations of authority.

They, poor deluded wretches, thought every danger of a restoration of the old system had passed away; and thus they made use of the whole of the old State machinery for the purpose of restoring "order." Not a single bureaucrat or military officer was dismissed; not the slightest change was made in the old bureaucratic system of administration. These precious constitutional and responsible ministers even restored to their posts those functionaries whom the people, in the first heat of revolutionary ardor, had driven away on account of their former acts of bureaucratic overbearing. There was nothing altered in Prussia but the persons of the ministers; even the ministerial staffs in the different departments were not touched upon, and all the constitutional place-hunters, who had formed the chorus of the newly-elevated rulers, and who had expected their share of power and office, were told to wait until restored stability allowed changes to be operated in the bureaucratic personnel which now were not without danger.

The King, chap-fallen in the highest degree after the insurrection of the 18th of March, very soon found out that he was quite as necessary to these "liberal" ministers as they were to him. The throne had been spared by the insurrection; the throne was the last existing obstacle to "anarchy"; the liberal middle class and its leaders, now in the ministry, had therefore every interest to keep on excellent terms with the crown. The King, and the reactionary camerilla that surrounded him, were not slow in discovering this, and profited by the circumstance in order to fetter the march of the ministry even in those petty reforms that were from time to time intended.

The first care of the ministry was to give a sort of legal appearance to the recent violent changes. The United Diet was convoked in spite of all popular opposition, in order to vote as the legal and constitutional organ of the people a new electoral law for the election of an Assembly, which was to agree with the crown upon a new constitution. The elections were to be indirect, the mass of voters electing a number of electors, who then were to choose the representative. In spite of all opposition this system of double elections passed. The United Diet was then asked for a loan of twenty-five millions of dollars, opposed by the popular party, but equally agreed to.

These acts of the ministry gave a most rapid development to the popular, or as it now called itself, the Democratic party. This party, headed by the petty trading and shopkeeping class, and uniting under its banner, in the beginning of the revolution, the large majority of the working people, demanded direct and universal suffrage, the same as established in France, a single legislative assembly, and full and open recognition of the revolution of the 18th of March, as the base of the new governmental system. The more moderate faction would be satisfied with a thus "democratized" monarchy, the more advanced demanded the ultimate establishment of the republic. Both factions agreed in recognizing the

German National Assembly at Frankfort as the supreme authority of the country, while the Constitutionalists and Reactionists affected a great horror of the sovereignty of this body, which they professed to consider as utterly revolutionary.

The independent movement of the working classes had, by the revolution, been broken up for a time. The immediate wants and circumstances of the movement were such as not to allow any of the specific demands of the Proletarian party to be put in the foreground. In fact, as long as the ground was not cleared for the independent action of the working men, as long as direct and universal suffrage was not yet established, as long as the thirty-six larger and smaller states continued to cut up Germany into numberless morsels, what else—could the Proletarian party do but watch the—for them all-important —movement of Paris, and struggle in common with the petty shopkeepers for the attainment of those rights, which would allow them to fight afterwards their own battle?

There were only three points, then, by which the Proletarian party in its political action essentially distinguished itself from the petty trading class, or properly so-called Democratic party; firstly, in judging differently the French movement, with regard to which the democrats attacked, and the Proletarian revolutionists defended, the extreme party in Paris; secondly, in proclaiming the necessity of establishing a German Republic, one and indivisible, while the very

extremest ultras among the democrats only dared
to sigh for a Federative Republic; and thirdly, in
showing upon every occasion, that revolutionary
boldness and readiness for action, in which any
party headed by, and composed principally of
petty tradesmen, will always be deficient.

The Proletarian, or really Revolutionary party,
succeeded only very gradually in withdrawing the
mass of the working people from the influence of
the Democrats, whose tail they formed in the
beginning of the Revolution. But in due time the
indecision, weakness, and cowardice of the Democratic leaders did the rest, and it may now be
said to be one of the principal results of the last
years' convulsions, that wherever the working-
class is concentrated in anything like considerable
masses, they are entirely freed from that Democratic influence which led them into an endless
series of blunders and misfortunes during 1848
and 1849. But we had better not anticipate; the
events of these two years will give us plenty of
opportunities to show the Democratic gentlemen
at work.

The peasantry in Prussia, the same as in Austria, but with less energy, feudalism pressing, upon the whole, not quite so hardly upon them here,
had profited by the revolution to free themselves
at once from all feudal shackles. But here, from
the reasons stated before, the middle classes at
once turned against them, their oldest, their most
indispensable allies; the democrats, equally
frightened with the bourgeoisie, by what was
called attacks upon private property, failed

equally to support them; and thus, after three months' emancipation, after bloody struggles and military executions, particularly in Silesia, feudalism was restored by the hands of the, until yesterday, anti-feudal bourgeoisie. There is not a more damning fact to be brought against them than this. Similar treason against its best allies, against itself, never was committed by any party in history, and whatever humiliation and chastisement may be in store for this middle class party, it has deserved by this one act every morsel of it.

OCTOBER, 1851.

VII.

THE FRANKFORT NATIONAL AS-
SEMBLY

February 27, 1852.

It will perhaps be in the recollection of our
readers that in the six preceding papers we followed up the revolutionary movement of Germany to the two great popular victories of March
13th in Vienna, and March 18th in Berlin. We
saw, both in Austria and Prussia, the establishment of constitutional governments and the proclamation, as leading rules for all future policy, of
Liberal, or middle class principles; and the only
difference observable between the two great centers of action was this, that in Prussia the liberal
bourgeoisie, in the persons of two wealthy merchants, Messrs. Camphausen and Hansemann, di-
rectly seized upon the reins of power; while in
Austria, where the bourgeoisie was, politically,
far less educated, the Liberal bureaucracy walked
into office, and professed to hold power in trust
for them. We have further seen, how the parties
and classes of society, that were heretofore all
united in opposition to the old government, got
divided among themselves after the victory, or

even during the struggle; and how that same Liberal bourgeoisie that alone profited from the victory turned round immediately upon its allies of yesterday, assumed a hostile attitude against every class or party of a more advanced character, and concluded an alliance with the conquered feudal and bureaucratic interests. It was in fact, evident, even from the beginning of the revolutionary drama, that the Liberal bourgeoisie could not hold its ground against the vanquished, but not destroyed, feudal and bureaucratic parties except by relying upon the assistance of the popular and more advanced parties; and that it equally required, against the torrent of these more advanced masses, the assistance of the feudal nobility and of the bureaucracy. Thus, it was clear enough that the bourgeoisie in Austria and Prussia did not possess sufficient strength to maintain their power, and to adapt the institutions of the country to their own wants and ideas. The Liberal bourgeois ministry was only a halting-place from which, according to the turn circumstances might take, the country would either have to go on to the more advanced stage of Unitarian republicanism, or to relapse into the old clerico-feudal and bureaucratic *régime*. At all events, the real, decisive struggle was yet to come; the events of March had only engaged the combat.

Austria and Prussia being the two ruling states of Germany, every decisive revolutionary victory in Vienna or Berlin would have been decisive for all Germany. And as far as they went,

the events of March, 1848, in these two cities,
decided the turn of German affairs.   It would,
then, be superfluous to recur to the movements
that occurred in the minor States; and we might,
indeed, confine ourselves to the consideration of
Austrian and Prussian affairs exclusively, if the
existence of these minor states had not given rise
to a body which was, by its very existence, a
most striking proof of the abnormal situation of
Germany and of the incompleteness of the late
revolution; a body so abnormal, so ludicrous by
its very position, and yet so full of its own importance, that history will, most likely, never afford a pendant to it.   This body was the so-called
German National Assembly at Frankfort-on-
Main.

   After the popular victories of Vienna and Berlin, it was a matter of course that there should
be a Representative Assembly for all Germany.
This body was consequently elected, and met at
Frankfort, by the side of the old Federative Diet.
The German National Assembly was expected,
by the people, to settle every matter in dispute,
and to act as the highest legislative authority for
the whole of the German Confederation.   But, at
the same time, the Diet which had convoked it
had in no way fixed its attributions.   No one
knew whether its decrees were to have force of
law, or whether they were to be subject to the
sanction of the Diet, or of the individual Governments.   In this perplexity, if the Assembly had
been possessed of the least energy, it would have
immediately dissolved and sent home the Diet—

than which no corporate body was more unpopular in Germany—and replaced it by a Federal Government, chosen from among its own members. It would have declared itself the only legal expression of the sovereign will of the German people, and thus have attached legal validity to every one of its decrees. It would, above all, have secured to itself an organized and armed force in the country sufficient to put down any opposition on the parts of the Governments. And all this was easy, very easy, at that early period of the Revolution. But that would have been expecting a great deal too much from an Assembly composed in its majority of Liberal attorneys and *doctrinaire* professors, an Assembly which, while it pretended to embody the very essence of German intellect and science, was in reality nothing but a stage where old and worn-out political characters exhibited their involuntary ludicrousness and their impotence of thought, as well as action, before the eyes of all Germany. THIS Assembly of old women was, from the first day of its existence, more frightened of the least popular movement than of all the reactionary plots of all the German Governments put together. It deliberated under the eyes of the Diet, nay, it almost craved the Diet's sanction to its decrees, for its first resolutions had to be promulgated by that odious body. Instead of asserting its own sovereignty, it studiously avoided the discussion of any such dangerous question. Instead of surrounding itself by a popular force, it passed to the order of the day over all the

violent encroachments of the Governments;
Mayence, under its very eyes, was placed in a
state of siege, and the people there disarmed,
and the National Assembly did not stir. Later
on it elected Archduke John of Austria Regent
of Germany, and declared that all its resolutions
were to have the force of law; but then Archduke John was only instituted in his new dignity
after the consent of all the Governments had been
obtained, and he was instituted not by the Assembly, but by the Diet; and as to the legal force
of the decrees of the Assembly, that point was
never recognized by the larger Governments, nor
enforced by the Assembly itself; it therefore remained in suspense. Thus we had the strange
spectacle of an Assembly pretending to be the
only legal representative of a great and sovereign nation, and yet never possessing either the
will or the force to make its claims recognized.
The debates of this body, without any practical
result, were not even of any theoretical value,
reproducing, as they did, nothing but the most
hackneyed commonplace themes of superannu-
ated philosophical and juridical schools; every
sentence that was said, or rather stammered
forth, in that Assembly having been printed a
thousand times over, and a thousand times better,
long before.

Thus the pretended new central authority of
Germany left everything as it had found it. So
far from realizing the long-demanded unity of
Germany, it did not dispossess the most insignificant of the princes who ruled her; it did not

draw closer the bonds of union between her separated provinces; it never moved a single step to
break down the customhouse barriers that separated Hanover from Prussia, and Prussia from
Austria; it did not even make the slightest attempt to remove the obnoxious dues that everywhere obstruct river navigation in Prussia. But
the less this Assembly did the more it blustered.
It created a German fleet—upon paper; it an-
nexed Poland and Schleswig; it allowed German-
Austria to carry on war against Italy, and yet
prohibited the Italians from following up the
Austrians into their safe retreat in Germany; it
gave three cheers and one cheer more for the
French republic, and it received Hungarian embassies, which certainly went home with far more
confused ideas about Germany than they had
come with.

This Assembly had been, in the beginning of
the Revolution, the bugbear of all German Governments. They had counted upon a very dic-
tatorial and revolutionary action on its part—on
account of the very want of definiteness in which
it had been found necessary to leave its compe-
tency. These Governments, therefore, got up a
most comprehensive system of intrigues in order
to weaken the influence of this dreaded body; but
they proved to have more luck than wits, for this
Assembly did the work of the Governments better
than they themselves could have done. The chief
feature among these intrigues was the convocation of local Legislative Assemblies, and in consequence, not only the lesser States convoked their

legislatures, but Prussia and Austria also called constituent assemblies. In these, as in the Frankfort House of Representatives, the Liberal middle class, or its allies, liberal lawyers, and bureaucrats had the majority, and the turn affairs took in each of them was nearly the same. The only difference is this, that the German National Assembly was the parliament of an imaginary country, as it had declined the task of forming what nevertheless was its own first condition of existence, viz. a United Germany; that it discussed the imaginary and never-to-be-carried-out measures of an imaginary government of its own creation, and that it passed imaginary resolutions for which nobody cared; while in Austria and Prussia the constituent bodies were at least real parliaments, upsetting and creating real ministries, and forcing, for a time at least, their resolutions upon the princes with whom they had to contend. They, too, were cowardly, and lacked enlarged views of revolutionary resolutions; they, too, betrayed the people, and restored power to the hands of feudal, bureaucratic, and military despotism. But then they were at least obliged to discuss practical questions of immediate interest, and to live upon earth with other people, while the Frankfort humbugs were never happier than when they could roam in "the airy realms of dream," *im Luftreich des Traums*. Thus the proceedings of the Berlin and Vienna Constituents form an important part of German revolutionary history, while the lucubrations of the Frankfort collective tomfoolery merely interest the collector of literary and antiquarian curiosities.

The people of Germany, deeply feeling the necessity of doing away with the obnoxious territorial division that scattered and annihilated the collective force of the nation, for some time expected to find, in the Frankfort National Assembly at least, the beginning of a new era. But the childish conduct of that set of wiseacres soon disenchanted the national enthusiasm. The disgraceful proceedings occasioned by the armistice of Malmoe (September, 1848,) made the popular indignation burst out against a body which, it had been hoped, would give the nation a fair field for action, and which, instead, carried away by unequalled cowardice, only restored to their former solidity the foundations upon which the present counter-revolutionary system is built.

LONDON, January, 1852.

VIII.

POLES, TSCHECHS, AND GERMANS.

FROM what has been stated in the foregoing articles, it is already evident that unless a fresh revolution was to follow that of March, 1848, things would inevitably return, in Germany, to what they were before this event. But such is the complicated nature of the historical theme upon which we are trying to throw some light, that subsequent events cannot be clearly understood without taking into account what may be called the foreign relations of the German Revolution. And these foreign relations were of the same intricate nature as the home affairs.

The whole of the eastern half of Germany, as far as the Elbe, Saale, and Bohemian Forest, has, it is well known, been reconquered during the last thousand years, from invaders of Slavonic origin. The greater part of these territories have been Germanized, to the perfect extinction of all Slavonic nationality and language, for several centuries past; and if we except a few totally isolated remnants, amounting in the aggregate to less than a hundred thousand souls (Kassubians in Pomerania, Wends or Sorbians in Lusatia)*, their inhabitants are, to all intents and purposes, Germans. But the case is different along the whole of the frontier of ancient Poland, and in the countries of the Tschechian tongue, in Bohemia and Moravia. Here the two nationalities are mixed up in every district, the towns being generally more or less German, while the Slavonic element prevails in the rural villages, where, however, it is also gradually disintegrated and forced back by the steady advance of German influence.

The reason of this state of things is this: ever since the time of Charlemagne, the Germans have directed their most constant and persevering efforts to the conquest, colonization, or, at least, civilization of the east of Europe. The conquest of the feudal nobility between the Elbe and the Oder, and the feudal colonies of the military orders of knights in Prussia and Livonia, only laid the ground for a far more extensive and effective system of Germanization by the trading and manufacturing middle classes, which in Germany, as in the rest of Western Europe, rose into social and political importance since the fifteenth century. The Slavonians, and particularly the Western Slavonians (Poles and Tschechs), are

---

*) Lusiana, an ancient territory of Germany, north of Bohemia, to which the whole of it originally belonged. Later it belonged to Saxony, and still later, in 1815, was divided between Saxony (the northern part) and Prussia (the southern).

essentially an agricultural race; trade and manufactures never were in great favor with them.
The consequence was that, with the increase of
population and the origin of cities in these regi-
ons, the production of all articles of manufac-
ture fell into the hands of German immigrants,
and the exchange of these commodities against
agricultural produce became the exclusive monopoly of the Jews, who, if they belong to any
nationality, are in these countries certainly rather
Germans than Slavonians. This has been, though
in a less degree, the case in all the east of Europe.
The handicraftsman, the small shopkeeper, the
petty manufacturer, is a German up to this day
in Petersburg, Pesth, Jassy, and even Constantinople; while the money-lender, the publican, the
hawker—a very important man in these thinly
populated countries—is very generally a Jew,
whose native tongue is a horribly corrupted German. The importance of the German element in
the Slavonic frontier localities, thus rising with
the growth of towns, trade and manufactures,
was still increased when it was found necessary
to import almost every element of mental culture
from Germany; after the German merchant and
handicraftsman, the German clergyman, the German schoolmaster, the German *savant* came to
establish himself upon Slavonic soil. And lastly,
the iron thread of conquering armies, or the
cautious, well-premeditated grasp of diplomacy,
not only followed, but many times went ahead
of the slow but sure advance of denationaliza-
tion by social development. Thus, great parts of

Western Prussia and Posen have been Germanized since the first partition of Poland, by sales
and grants of public domains to German colon-
ists, by encouragements given to German capitalists for the establishment of manufactories,
etc., in those neighborhoods, and very often, too,
by excessively despotic measures against the Polish inhabitants of the country.

In this manner the last seventy years had entirely changed the line of demarcation between
the German and Polish nationalities. The Revolution of 1848 calling forth at once the claim of
all oppressed nations to an independent existence,
and to the right of settling their own affairs for
themselves, it was quite natural that the Poles
should at once demand the restoration of their
country within the frontiers of the old Polish
Republic before 1772. It is true, this frontier,
even at that time, had become obsolete, if taken
as the delimitation of German and Polish nationality; it had become more so every year since by
the progress of Germanization; but then, the
Germans had proclaimed such an enthusiasm for
the restoration of Poland, that they must expect
to be asked, as a first proof of the reality of their
sympathies to give up *their* share of the plunder.
On the other hand, should whole tracts of land,
inhabited chiefly by Germans, should large towns,
entirely German, be given up to a people that as
yet had never given any proofs of its capability
of progressing beyond a state of feudalism based
upon agricultural serfdom? The question was
intricate enough. The only possible solution was

in a war with Russia. The question of delimitation between the different revolutionized nations would have been made a secondary one to that of first establishing a safe frontier against the common enemy. The Poles, by receiving extended territories in the east, would have become more tractable and reasonable in the west; and Riga and Milan would have been deemed, after all, quite as important to them as Danzig and Elbing. Thus the advanced party in Germany, deeming a war with Russia necessary to keep up the Continental movement, and considering that the national re-establishment even of a part of Poland would inevitably lead to such a war, supported the Poles; while the reigning middle class partly clearly foresaw its downfall from any national war against Russia, which would have called more active and energetic men to the helm, and, therefore, with a feigned enthusiasm for the extension of German nationality, they declared Prussian Poland, the chief seat of Polish revolutionary agitation, to be part and parcel of the German Empire that was to be. The promises given to the Poles in the first days of excitement were shamefully broken. Polish armaments got up with the sanction of the Government were dispersed and massacred by Prussian artillery; and as soon as the month of April, 1848, within six weeks of the Berlin Revolution, the Polish movement was crushed, and the old national hostility revived between Poles and Germans. This immense and incalculable service to the Russian autocrat was performed by the Liberal merchant-ministers, Camphausen and Hansemann. It must be added that this Polish campaign was the first means of reorganizing and reassuring that same Prussian army, which afterward turned out the Liberal party, and crushed the movement which Messrs. Camphausen and Hansemann had taken such pains to bring about. "Whereby they sinned, thereby are they punished." Such has been the fate of all the upstarts of 1848 and 1849, from Ledru Rolin to Changarnier, and from Camphausen down to Haynau.

The question of nationality gave rise to another struggle in Bohemia. This country, inhabited by two millions of Germans, and three millions of Slavonians of the Tschechian tongue, had great historical recollections, almost all connected with the former supremacy of the Tschechs. But then the force of this branch of the Slavonic family had been broken ever since the wars of the Hussites in the fifteenth century. The province speaking the Tschechian tongue was divided, one part forming the kingdom of Bohemia, another the principality of Moravia, a third the Carpathian hill-country of the Slovaks, being part of Hungary. The Moravians and Slovaks had long since lost every vestige of national feeling and vitality, although mostly preserving their language. Bohemia was surrounded by thoroughly German countries on three sides out of four. The German element had made great progress on her own territory; even in the capital, in Prague, the two nationalities were pretty equally matched; and everywhere capital, trade, industry, and mental culture were in the hands of the Germans. The chief champion of the Tschechian nationality, Professor Palacky, is himself nothing but a learned German run mad, who even now cannot speak the Tschechian language correctly and without foreign accent. But as it often happens, dying Tschechian nationality, dying according to every fact known in history for the last four hundred years, made in 1848 a last effort to regain its former vitality—an effort whose failure, independently of all revolutionary considerations, was to prove that Bohemia could only exist, henceforth, as a portion of Germany, although part of her inhabitants might yet, for some centuries, continue to speak a non-German language.

LONDON, February, 1852.

IX.

PANSLAVISM—THE SCHLESWIG-HOLSTEIN WAR.

March 15th, 1852.

BOHEMIA and Croatia (another disjected member of the Slavonic family, acted upon by the Hungarian, as Bohemia by the German) were the homes of what is called on the European continent "Panslavism." Neither Bohemia nor Croatia was strong enough to exist as a nation by herself. Their respective nationalities, gradually undermined by the action of historical causes that inevitably absorbs into a more energetic stock, could only hope to be restored to anything like independence by an alliance with other Slavonic nations. There were twenty-two millions of Poles, forty-five millions of Russians, eight millions of Serbians and Bulgarians; why not form a mighty confederation of the whole eighty millions of Slavonians, and drive back or exterminate the intruder upon the holy Slavonic soil, the Turk, the Hungarian, and above all the hated, but indispensable *Niemetz,* the German? Thus in the studies of a few Slavonian *dilettanti* of historical science was this ludicrous, this anti-historical movement got up, a movement which intended nothing less than to subjugate the civilized West under the barbarian East, the town under the country, trade, manufactures, intelligence, under the primitive agriculture of Slavonian serfs. But behind this ludicrous theory stood the terrible reality of the *Russian Empire;* that empire which by every movement proclaims the pretension of considering all Europe as the domain of the Slavonic race, and especially of the only energetic part of this race, of the Russians; that empire which, with two capitals such as St. Peterburg and Moscow, has not yet found its centre of gravity, as long as the "City of the Czar" (Constantinople, called in Russian Tzarigrad, the Czar's city), considered by every Russian peasant as the true metropolis of his religion and his nation, is not actually the residence of its Emperor; that empire which, for the last one hundred and fifty years, has never lost, but always gained territory by every war it has commenced. And well known in Central Europe are the intrigues by which Russian policy supported the new-fangled system of Panslavism, a system than which none better could be invented to suit its purposes. Thus, the Bohemian and Croatian Panslavists, some intentionally, some without knowing it, worked in the direct interest of Russia; they betrayed the revolutionary cause for the shadow of a nationality which, in the best of cases, would have shared the fate of the Polish nationality under Russian sway. It must, however, be said for the honor of the Poles, that they never got to be seriously entangled in these Panslavist traps, and if a few of the aristocracy turned furious Panslavists, they knew that by Russian subjugation they had less to lose than by a revolt of their own peasant serfs.

The Bohemians and Croatians called, then, a general Slavonic Congress at Prague, for the preparation of the universal Slavonian Alliance. This Congress would have proved a decided failure even without the interference of the Austrian military. The several Slavonic languages differ quite as much as the English, the German, and the Swedish, and when the proceedings opened, there was no common Slavonic tongue by which the speakers could make themselves understood. French was tried, but was equally unintelligible to the majority, and the poor Slavonic enthusiasts, whose only common feeling was a common hatred against the Germans, were at last obliged to express themselves in the hated German language, as the only one that was generally understood! But just then another Slavonic Congress was assembling in Prague, in the shape of Galician lancers, Croatian and Slovak grenadiers, and Bohemian gunners and cuirassiers; and this real, armed Slavonic Congress, under the command of Windischgrätz, in less than twenty-four hours drove the founders of an imaginary Slavonian supremacy out of the town, and dispersed them to the winds.

The Bohemian, Moravian, Dalmatian, and part of the Polish deputies (the aristocracy) to the

Austrian Constituent Diet, made in that Assembly a systematic war upon the German element. The Germans, and part of the Poles (the impoverished nobility), were in this Assembly the chief supporters of revolutionary progress; the mass of the Slavonic deputies, in opposing them, were not satisfied with thus showing clearly the reactionary tendencies of their entire movement, but they were degraded enough to tamper and conspire with the very same Austrian Government which had dispersed their meeting at Prague. They, too, were paid for this infamous conduct; after supporting the Government during the insurrection of October, 1848, an event which finally secured to them a majority in the Diet, this now almost exclusively Slavonic Diet was dispersed by Austrian soldiers, the same as the Prague Congress, and the Panslavists threatened with imprisonment if they should stir again. And they have only obtained this, that Slavonic nationality is now being everywhere undermined by Austrian centralization, a result for which they may thank their own fanaticism and blindness.

If the frontiers of Hungary and Germany had admitted of any doubt, there would certainly have been another quarrel there. But, fortunately, there was no pretext, and the interests of both nations being intimately related, they struggled against the same enemies, *viz.*, the Austrian Government and the Panslavistic fanaticism. The good understanding was not for a moment disturbed. But the Italian Revolution entangled at least a part of Germany in an internecine war, and it must be stated here, as a proof how far the Metternichian system had succeeded in keeping back the development of the public mind, that during the first six months of 1848, the same men that had in Vienna mounted the barricades, went, full of enthusiasm, to join the army that fought against the Italian patriots. This deplorable confusion of ideas did not, however, last long.

Lastly, there was the war with Denmark about Schleswig and Holstein. These countries, unquestionably German by nationality, language and predilection, are also from military, naval and commercial grounds necessary to Germany. Their inhabitants have, for the last three years, struggled hard against Danish intrusion. The right of treaties, besides, was for them. The Revolution of March brought them into open collision with the Danes, and Germany supported them. But while in Poland, in Italy, in Bohemia, and later on, in Hungary, military operations were pushed with the utmost vigor, in this the only popular, the only, at least partially, revolutionary war, a system of resultless marches and counter-marches was adopted, and an interference of foreign diplomacy was submitted to, which led, after many an heroic engagement, to a most miserable end. The German Government betrayed, during the war, the Schleswig-Holstein revolutionary army on every occasion, and allowed it purposely to be cut up, when dispersed or divided, by the Danes. The German corps of volunteers were treated the same.

But while thus the German name earned nothing but hatred on every side, the German Constitutional and Liberal Governments rubbed their
hands for joy. They had succeeded in crushing
the Polish and the Bohemian movements. They
had everywhere revived the old national animos-
ities, which heretofore had prevented any common understanding and action between the German, the Pole, the Italian. They had accustomed
the people to scenes of civil war and repression
by the military. The Prussian army had regained
its confidence in Poland, the Austrian army in
Prague; and while the superabundant patriotism
(*"die Patriotische Ueberkraft,"* as Heine has it)
of revolutionary but short-sighted youth was led
in Schleswig and Lombardy, to be crushed by
the grape-shot of the enemy, the regular army,
the real instrument of action, both of Prussia
and Austria, was placed in a position to regain
public favor by victories over the foreigner.
But we repeat: these armies, strengthened by the
Liberals as a means of action against the more
advanced party, no sooner had recovered their
self-confidence and their discipline in some degree, than they turned themselves against the
Liberals, and restored to power the men of the
old system. When Radetzky, in his camp beyond
the Adige, received the first orders from the
"responsible ministers" at Vienna, he exclaimed:
"Who are these ministers? They are not the
Government of Austria! Austria is now nowhere
but in my camp; I and my army, we are Austria;
and when we shall have beaten the Italians we

shall reconquer the Empire for the Emperor!" And old Radetzky was right—but the imbecile "responsible" ministers at Vienna heeded him not.

LONDON, February, 1852.

X.

THE PARIS RISING—THE FRANKFORT ASSEMBLY.

MARCH 18th, 1852.

As early as the beginning of April, 1848, the revolutionary torrent had found itself stemmed all over the Continent of Europe by the league which those classes of society that had profited by the first victory immediately formed with the vanquished. In France, the petty trading class and the Republican faction of the bourgeoisie had combined with the Monarchist bourgeoisie against the proletarians; in Germany and Italy, the victorious bourgeoisie had eagerly courted the support of the feudal nobility, the official bureaucracy, and the army, against the mass of the people and the petty traders. Very soon the united Conservative and Counter-Revolutionary parties again regained the ascendant. In England, an untimely and ill-prepared popular demonstration (April 10th) turned out a complete and decisive defeat of the popular party. In France, two similar movements (16th April and 15th May) were equally defeated. In Italy, King

Bomba regained his authority by a single stroke on the 15th May. In Germany, the different new bourgeois Governments and their respective constituent Assemblies consolidated themselves, and if the eventful 15th of May gave rise, in Vienna, to a popular victory, this was an event of merely secondary importance, and may be considered the last successful flash of popular energy. In Hungary the movement appeared to turn into the quiet channel of perfect legality, and the Polish movement, as we have seen in our last, was stifled in the bud by Prussian bayonets. But as yet nothing was decided as to the eventual turn which things would take, and every inch of ground lost by the Revolutionary parties in the different countries only tended to close their ranks more and more for the decisive action.

The decisive action drew near. It could be fought in France only; for France, as long as England took no part in the revolutionary strife, or as Germany remained divided, was, by its national independence, civilization, and centralization, the only country to impart the impulse of a mighty convulsion to the surrounding countries. Accordingly, when, on the 23rd of June, 1848, the bloody struggle began in Paris, when every succeeding telegraph or mail more clearly exposed the fact to the eyes of Europe, that this struggle was carried on between the mass of the working people on the one hand, and all the other classes of the Parisian population, supported by the army, on the other; when the fighting went on for several days with an exasperation unequalled in the history of modern civil warfare, but without any apparent advantage for either side—then it became evident to every one that this was the great decisive battle which would, if the insurrection were victorious, deluge the whole continent with renewed revolutions, or, if it was suppressed, bring about an at least momentary restoration of counter-revolutionary rule.

The proletarians of Paris were defeated, decimated, crushed with such an effect that even now they have not yet recovered from the blow. And immediately, all over Europe, the new and old Conservatives and Counter-Revolutionists raised their heads with an effrontery that showed how well they understood the importance of the event. The Press was everywhere attacked, the rights of meeting and association were interfered with, every little event in every small provincial town was taken profit of to disarm the people to declare a state of siege, to drill the troops in the new manœuvres and artifices that Cavaignac had taught them. Besides, for the first time since February, the invincibility of a popular insurrection in a large town had been proved to be a delusion; the honor of the armies had been restored; the troops hitherto always defeated in street battles of importance regained confidence in their efficiency even in this kind of struggle.

From this defeat of the *ouvriers* of Paris may be dated the first positive steps and definite plans of the old feudal bureaucratic party in Germany, to get rid even of their momentary allies, the middle classes, and to restore Germany to the state she was in before the events of March. The army again was the decisive power in the State, and the army belonged not to the middle classes but to themselves. Even in Prussia, where before 1848 a considerable leaning of part of the lower grades of officers towards a Constitutional Government had been observed, the disorder introduced into the army by the Revolution had brought back those reasoning young men to their allegiance; as soon as the private soldier took a few liberties with regard to the officers, the necessity of discipline and passive obedience became at once strikingly evident to them. The vanquished nobles and bureaucrats now began to see their way before them; the army, more united than ever, flushed with victory in minor insurrections and in foreign warfare, jealous of the great success the French soldiers had just attained—this army had only to be kept in constant petty conflicts with the people, and the decisive moment once at hand, it could with one great blow crush the Revolutionists, and set aside the presumptions of the middle class Parliamentarians. And the proper moment for such a decisive blow arrived soon enough.

We pass over the sometimes curious, but mostly tedious, parliamentary proceedings and local struggles that occupied, in Germany, the different parties during the summer. Suffice it to say that the supporters of the middle class interest in spite of numerous parliamentary triumphs, not one of which led to any practical result, very generally felt that their position between the extreme parties became daily more untenable, and that, therefore, they were obliged now to seek the alliance of the reactionists, and the next day to court the favor of the more popular factions. This constant vacillation gave the finishing stroke to their character in public opinion, and according to the turn events were taking, the contempt into which they had sunk, profited for the movement principally to the bureaucrats and feudalists.

By the beginning of autumn the relative position of the different parties had become exasperated and critical enough to make a decisive battle inevitable. The first engagements in this war between the democratic and revolutionary masses and the army took place at Frankfort. Though a mere secondary engagement, it was the first advantage of any note the troops acquired over the insurrection, and had a great moral effect. The fancy Government established by the Frankfort National Assembly had been allowed by Prussia, for very obvious reasons, to conclude an armistice with Denmark, which not only surrendered to Danish vengeance the Germans of Schleswig, but which also entirely disclaimed the more or less revolutionary principles which were generally supposed in the Danish war. This armistice was, by a majority of two or three, rejected in the Frankfort Assembly. A sham ministerial crisis followed this vote, but three days later the Assembly reconsidered their vote, and were actually induced to cancel it and acknowledge the armistice. This disgraceful proceeding roused the indignation of the people. Barricades were erected, but already sufficient troops had been drawn to Frankfort, and after six hours' fighting, the insurrection was suppressed. Similar, but less important, movements connected with this event took place in other parts of Germany (Baden, Cologne), but were equally defeated.

This preliminary engagement gave to the Counter-Revolutionary party the one great advantage, that now the only Government which had entirely—at least in semblance—originated with popular election, the Imperial Government of Frankfort, as well as the National Assembly, was ruined in the eyes of the people. This Government and this Assembly had been obliged to appeal to the bayonets of the troops against the manifestation of the popular will. They were compromised, and what little regard they might have been hitherto enabled to claim, this repudiation of their origin, the dependency upon the anti-popular Governments and their troops, made both the Lieutenant of the Empire, his ministers and his deputies, henceforth to be complete nullities. We shall soon see how first Austria, then Prussia, and later on the smaller States too, treated with contempt every order, every request, every deputation they received from this body of impotent dreamers.

We now come to the great counter-stroke in Germany, of the French battle of June, to that event which was as decisive for Germany as the proletarian struggle of Paris had been for

France; we mean the revolution and subsequent storming of Vienna, October, 1848. But the importance of this battle is such, and the explanation of the different circumstances that more immediately contributed to its issue will take up such a portion of *The Tribune's* columns, as to necessitate its being treated in a separate letter.

LONDON, February, 1852.

XI.

THE VIENNA INSURRECTION.

MARCH 19th, 1852.

WE now come to the decisive event which formed the counter-revolutionary part in Germany to the Parisian insurrection of June, and which, by a single blow, turned the scale in favor of the Counter-Revolutionary party,—the insurrection of October, 1848, in Vienna.

We have seen what the position of the different classes was, in Vienna, after the victory of 12th March. We have also seen how the movement of German-Austria was entangled with and impeded by the events in the non-German provinces of Austria. It only remains for us, then, briefly to survey the causes which led to this last and most formidable rising of German-Austria.

The high aristocracy and the stock-jobbing bourgeoisie, which had formed the principal non-official supports of the Metternichian Government, were enabled, even after the events of March, to maintain a predominating influence with the Government, not only by the Court, the army and the bureaucracy, but still more by the horror of "anarchy," which rapidly spread among the middle classes. They very soon ventured a few feelers in the shape of a Press Law, a non-descript Aristocratic Constitution, and an Electoral Law based upon the old division of "estates." The so-called Constitutional ministry, consisting of half Liberal, timid, incapable bureaucrats, on the 14th of May, even ventured a direct attack upon the revolutionary organizations of the masses by dissolving the Central Committee of Delegates of the National Guard and Academic Legion, a body formed for the express purpose of controlling the Government, and calling out against it, in case of need, the popular forces. But this act only provoked the insurrection of the 15th May, by which the Government was forced to acknowledge the Committee, to repeal the Constitution and the Electoral Law and to grant the power of framing a new Fundamental Law to a Constitutional Diet, elected by universal suffrage. All this was confirmed on the following day by an Imperial proclamation. But the reactionary party, which also had its representatives in the ministry, soon got their "Liberal" colleagues to undertake a new attack upon the popular conquests. The Academic Legion, the stronghold of the movement party, the centre of continuous agitation, had, on this very account, become obnoxious to the more moderate burghers of Vienna; on the 26th a ministerial decree dissolved it. Perhaps this blow might have succeeded, if it had been carried out by a part of the National Guard only, but the Government, not trusting them either, brought the military forward, and at once the National Guard turned round, united with the Academic Legion, and thus frustrated the ministerial project.

In the meantime, however, the Emperor and his Court had, on the 16th of May, left Vienna, and fled to Innspruck. Here surrounded by the bigoted Tyroleans, whose loyalty was roused again by the danger of an invasion of their country by the Sardo-Lombardian army, supported by the vicinity of Radetzky's troops, within shell-range of whom Innspruck lay, here the Counter-Revolutionary party found an asylum, from whence, uncontrolled, unobserved and safe, it might rally its scattered forces, repair and spread again all over the country the network of its plots. Communications were reopened with Radetzky, with Jellachich, and with Windischgrätz, as well as with the reliable men in the administrative hierarchy of the different provinces; intrigues were set on foot with the Slavonic chiefs, and thus a real force at the disposal of the Counter-Revolutionary camarilla was formed, while the impotent ministers in Vienna were allowed to wear their short and feeble popularity out in continual bickerings with the revolutionary masses, and in the debates of the forthcoming Constituent Assembly. Thus the policy of leaving the movement of the capital to itself for a time; a policy which must have led to the omnipotence of the movement party in a centralized and homogeneous country like France, here in Austria, in a heterogeneous political conglomerate, was one of the safest means of reorganizing the strength of the reactionists.

In Vienna the middle class, persuaded that after three successive defeats, and in the face of a Constituent Assembly based upon universal suffrage, the Court was no longer an opponent to be dreaded, fell more and more into that weariness and apathy, and that eternal outcry for order and tranquillity, which has everywhere seized this class after violent commotions and consequent derangement of trade. The manufactures of the Austrian capital are almost exclusively limited to articles of luxury, for which, since the Revolution and the flight of the Court, there had necessarily been little demand. The shout for a return to a regular system of government, and for a return of the Court, both of which were expected to bring about a revival of commercial prosperity—this shout became now general among the middle classes. The meeting of the Constituent Assembly in July was hailed with delight as the end of the revolutionary era; so was the return of the Court, which, after the victories of Radetzky in Italy, and after the advent of the reactionary ministry of Doblhoff, considered itself strong enough to brave the popular torrent, and which, at the same time, was wanted in Vienna in order to complete its intrigues with the Slavonic majority of the Diet. While the Constituent Diet discussed the laws on the emancipation of the peasantry from feudal bondage and forced labor for the nobility, the Court completed a master stroke. On the 19th

of August the Emperor was made to review the
National Guard; the Imperial family, the court-
iers, the general officers, outbade each other in
flatteries to the armed burghers, who were already intoxicated with pride at thus seeing themselves publicly acknowledged as one of the important bodies of the State; and immediately afterwards a decree, signed by Herr Schwarzer,
the only popular minister in the Cabinet, was
published, withdrawing the Government aid,
given hitherto to the workmen out of employ.
The trick succeeded; the working classes got up
a demonstration; the middle class National
Guards declared for the decree of their minister;
they were launched upon the "Anarchists," fell
like tigers on the unarmed and unresisting work-
people, and massacred a great number of them
on the 23rd of August. Thus the unity and
strength of the revolutionary force was broken;
the class-struggle between bourgeois and proletarian had come in Vienna, too, to a bloody outbreak, and the counter-revolutionary camarilla
saw the day approaching on which it might strike
its grand blow.

The Hungarian affairs very soon offered an
opportunity to proclaim openly the principles
upon which it intended to act. On the 5th of
October an Imperial decree in the *Vienna Gazette*
—a decree countersigned by none of the responsible ministers for Hungary—declared the Hungarian Diet dissolved, and named the Ban Jellachich, of Croatia, civil and military governor
of that country—Jellachich, the leader of South

Slavonian reaction, a man who was actually at war with the lawful authorities of Hungary. At the same time orders were given to the troops in Vienna to march out and form part of the army which was to enforce Jellachich's authority. This, however, was showing the cloven foot too openly; every man in Vienna felt that war upon Hungary was war upon the principle of constitutional government, which principle was in the very decree trampled upon by the attempt of the emperor to make decrees with legal force, without the countersign of a responsible minister. The people, the Academic Legion, the National Guard of Vienna, on the 6th of October rose in mass, and resisted the departure of the troops; some grenadiers passed over to the people; a short struggle took place between the popular forces and the troops; the minister of war, Latour, was massacred by the people, and in the evening the latter were victors. In the meantime, Ban Jellachich, beaten at Stuhlweissenburg by Perczel, had taken refuge near Vienna on German-Austrian territory; the Viennese troops that were to march to his support now took up an ostensibly hostile and defensive position against him; and the emperor and court had again fled to Olmütz, on semi-Slavonic territory.

But at Olmütz the Court found itself in very different circumstances from what it had been at Innspruck. It was now in a position to open immediately the campaign against the Revolution. It was surrounded by the Slavonian deputies of the Constituent, who flocked in masses to

Olmütz, and by the Slavonian enthusiasts from all parts of the monarchy. The campaign, in their eyes, was to be a war of Slavonian restoration and of extermination, against the two intruders, upon what was considered Slavonian soil, against the German and the Magyar. Windischgrätz, the conqueror of Prague, now commander of the army that was concentrated around Vienna, became at once the hero of Slavonian nationality. And his army concentrated rapidly from all sides. From Bohemia, Moravia, Styria, Upper Austria, and Italy, marched regiment after regiment on routes that converged at Vienna, to join the troops of Jellachich and the ex-garrison of the capital. Above sixty thousand men were thus united towards the end of October, and soon they commenced hemming in the imperial city on all sides, until, on the 30th of October, they were far enough advanced to venture upon the decisive attack.

In Vienna, in the meantime, confusion and helplessness was prevalent. The middle class, as soon as the victory was gained, became again possessed of their old distrust against the "anarchic" working classes; the working men, mindful of the treatment they had received, six weeks before, at the hands of the armed tradesmen, and of the unsteady, wavering policy of the middle class at large, would not trust to them the defence of the city, and demanded arms and military organization for themselves. The Academic Legion, full of zeal for the struggle against imperial despotism, were entirely incapable of understanding the nature of the estrangement of the two classes, or of otherwise comprehending the necessities of the situation. There was confusion in the public mind, confusion in the ruling councils. The remnant of the German Diet deputies, and a few Slavonians, acting the part of spies for their friends at Olmütz, besides a few of the more revolutionary Polish deputies, sat in permanency; but instead of taking part resolutely, they lost all their time in idle debates upon the possibility of resisting the imperial army without overstepping the bounds of constitutional conventionalities. The committee of safety, composed of deputies from almost all the popular bodies of Vienna, although resolved to resist, was yet dominated by a majority of burghers and petty tradesmen, who never allowed it to follow up any determined, energetic line of action. The council of the Academic Legion passed heroic resolutions, but was in no way able to take the lead. The working classes, distrusted, disarmed, disorganized, hardly emerging from the intellectual bondage of the old *régime,* hardly awaking, not to a knowledge, but to a mere instinct of their social position and proper political line of action, could only make themselves heard by loud demonstrations, and could not be expected to be up to the difficulties of the moment. But they were ready—as they ever were in Germany during the revolution—to fight to the last, as soon as they obtained arms.

That was the state of things in Vienna. Outside, the reorganized Austrian army flushed with the victories of Radetzky in Italy; sixty or seventy thousand men well armed, well organized, and if not well commanded at least possessing commanders. Inside, confusion, class division, disorganization; a national guard part of which was resolved not to fight at all, part irresolute, and only the smallest part ready to act; a proletarian mass, powerful by numbers but without leaders, without any political education, subject to panic as well as to fits of fury almost without cause, a prey to every false rumor spread about, quite ready to fight, but unarmed, at least in the beginning, and incompletely armed, and barely organized when at last they were led to battle; a helpless Diet, discussing theoretical quibbles while the roof over their heads was almost burning; a leading committee without impulse or energy. Everything was changed from the days of March and May, when, in the counter-revolutionary camp, all was confusion, and when the only organized force was that created by the revolution. There could hardly be a doubt about the issue of such a struggle, and whatever doubt there might be, was settled by the events of the 30th and 31st of October, and 1st November.

LONDON, March, 1852.

XII.

THE STORMING OF VIENNA—THE BETRAYAL OF VIENNA.

APRIL 9th, 1852.

WHEN at last the concentrated army of Windischgrätz commenced the attack upon Vienna, the forces that could be brought forward in defence were exceedingly insufficient for the purpose. Of the National Guard only a portion was to be brought to the entrenchments. A Proletarian Guard, it is true, had at last been hastily formed, but owing to the lateness of the attempt to thus make available the most numerous, most daring, and most energetic part of the population, it was too little inured to the use of arms and to the very first rudiments of discipline to offer a successful resistance. Thus the Academic Legion, three to four thousand strong, well exercised and disciplined to a certain degree, brave and enthusiastic, was, militarily speaking, the only force which was in a state to do its work successfully. But what were they, together with the few reliable National Guards, and with the confused mass of the armed proletarians, in opposition to the far more numerous regulars of Windischgrätz, not counting even the brigand hordes of Jellachich, hordes that were, by the very nature of their habits, very useful in a war from house to house, from lane to lane? And what but a few old, outworn, ill-mounted, and ill-served pieces of ordnance had the insurgents to oppose to that numerous and well-appointed artillery, of which Windischgrätz made such an unscrupulous use?

The nearer the danger drew, the more grew the confusion in Vienna. The Diet, up to the last moment, could not collect sufficient energy to call in for aid the Hungarian army of Perczel, encamped a few leagues below the capital. The committee passed contradictory resolutions, they themselves being, like the popular armed masses, floated up and down with the alternately rising and receding tide of rumors and counter-rumors. There was only one thing upon which all agreed —to respect property; and this was done in a degree almost ludicrous for such times. As to the final arrangement of a plan of defence, very little was done. Bem, the only man present who could have saved Vienna, if any could then in Vienna, an almost unknown foreigner, a Slavonian by birth, gave up the task, overwhelmed as he was by universal distrust. Had he persevered, he might have been lynched as a traitor. Messenhauser, the commander of the insurgent forces, more of a novel-writer than even of a subaltern officer, was totally inadequate to the task; and yet, after eight months of revolutionary struggles, the popular party had not produced or acquired a military man of more ability than he. Thus the contest began. The Viennese considering their utterly inadequate means of defence, considering their utter absence of military skill and organization in the ranks, offered a most heroic resistance. In many places the order given by Bem, when he was in command, "to defend that post to the last man," was carried out to the letter. But force prevailed. Barricade after barricade was swept away by the imperial artillery in the long and wide avenues which form the main streets of the suburbs; and on the evening of the second day's fighting the Croats occupied the range of houses facing the glacis of the Old Town. A feeble and disorderly attack of the Hungarian army had been utterly defeated; and during an armistice, while some parties in the Old Town capitulated, while others hesitated and spread confusion, while the remnants of the Academic Legion prepared fresh intrenchments, an entrance was made by the imperialists, and in the midst of the general disorder the Old Town was carried.

The immediate consequences of this victory, the brutalities and executions by martial law, the unheard-of cruelties and infamies committed by the Slavonian hordes let loose upon Vienna, are too well known to be detailed here. The ulterior consequences, the entirely new turn given to German affairs by the defeat of the revolution in Vienna, we shall have reason to notice hereafter. There remain two points to be considered in connection with the storming of Vienna. The people of that capital had two allies—the Hungarians and the German people. Where were they in the hour of trial?

We have seen that the Viennese, with all the generosity of a newly freed people, had risen for a cause which, though ultimately their own, was in the first instance, and above all, that of the Hungarians. Rather than suffer the Austrian troops to march upon Hungary, they would draw their first and most terrific onslaught upon themselves. And while they thus nobly came forward for the support of their allies, the Hungarians, successful against Jellachich, drove him upon Vienna, and by their victory strengthened the force that was to attack that town. Under these circumstances it was the clear duty of Hungary to support, without delay, and with all disposable forces, not the Diet of Vienna, not the Committee of Safety or any other official body at Vienna, but the *Viennese* revolution. And if Hungary should even have forgotten that Vienna had fought the first battle of Hungary, she owed it to her own safety not to forget that Vienna was the only outpost of Hungarian independence, and that after the fall of Vienna nothing could meet the advance of the imperial troops against herself. Now, we know very well all the Hungarians can say and have said in defence of their inactivity during the blockade and storming of Vienna: the insufficient state of their own force, the refusal of the Diet or any other official body in Vienna to call them in, the necessity to keep on constitutional ground, and to avoid complications with the German central power. But the fact is, as to the insufficient state of the Hungarian army, that in the first days after the Viennese revolution and the arrival of Jellachich, nothing was wanted in the shape of regular troops, as the Austrian regulars were very far from being concentrated; and that a courageous, unrelenting following up of the first advantage over Jellachich, even with nothing but the *Land Sturm* that had fought at Stuhlweissenburg, would have sufficed to effect a junction with the Viennese, and to adjourn to that day six months every concentration of an Austrian army. In war, and particularly in revolutionary warfare, rapidity of action until some decided advantage is gained is the first rule, and we have no hesitation in saying that upon *merely military grounds*. Perczel ought not to have stopped until his junction with the Viennese was affected. There was certainly some risk, but who ever won a battle without risking something? And did the people of Vienna risk nothing when they drew upon themselves— they, a population of four hundred thousand— the forces that were to march to the conquest of twelve millions of Hungarians? The military fault committed by waiting until the Austrians had united, and by making the feeble demonstration at Schwechat which ended, as it deserved to do, in an inglorious defeat—this military fault certainly incurred more risks than a resolute march upon Vienna against the disbanded brigands of Jellachich would have done.

But, it is said, such an advance of the Hungarians, unless authorized by some official body, would have been a violation of the German territory, would have brought on complications with the central power at Frankfort, and would have been, above all, an abandonment of the legal and constitutional policy which formed the strength of the Hungarian cause. Why, the official bodies in Vienna were nonentities! Was it the Diet, was it the popular committees, who had risen for Hungary, or was it the people of Vienna, and they alone, who had taken to the musket to stand the brunt of the first battle for Hungary's independence? It was not this nor that official body in Vienna which it was important to uphold; all these bodies might, and would have been, upset very soon in the progress of the revolutionary development; but it was the ascendancy of the revolutionary movement, the unbroken progress of popular action itself, which alone was in question, and which alone could save Hungary from invasion. What forms this revolutionary movement afterwards might take, was the business of the Viennese, not of the Hungarians, so long as Vienna and German Austria at large continued their allies against the common enemy. But the question is, whether in this stickling of the Hungarian government for some quasi-legal authorization, we are not to see the first clear symptom of that pretence to a rather doubtful legality of proceeding, which, if it did not save Hungary, at least told very well, at a later period, before the English middle class audiences.

As to the pretext of possible conflicts with the central power of Germany at Frankfort, it is quite futile. The Frankfort authorities were *de facto* upset by the victory of the counter-revolution at Vienna; they would have been equally upset had the revolution there found the support necessary to defeat its enemies. And lastly, the great argument that Hungary could not leave legal and **constitutional** ground, may do very well for British free-traders, but it will never be deemed sufficient in the eyes of history. Suppose the people of Vienna had stuck to "legal and constitutional means" on the 13th of March, and on the 6th of October, what then of the "legal and constitutional" movement, and of all the glorious battles which, for the first time, brought Hungary to the notice of the civilized world? The very legal and constitutional ground upon which it is asserted the Hungarians moved in 1848 and 1849 was conquered for them by the exceedingly illegal and unconstitutional rising of the people of Vienna on the 13th March. It is not to our purpose here to discuss the revolutionary history of Hungary, but it may be deemed proper if we observe that it is utterly useless to professedly use merely legal means of resistance against an enemy who scorns such scruples; and if we add, that had it not been for this eternal pretence of legality which Görgey seized upon and turned against the Government, the devotion of Görgey's army to its general, and the disgraceful catostrophe of Villagos, would have been impossible. And when, at last, to save their honor, the Hun-

garians came across the Leitha, in the latter end
of October, 1848, was not this quite as illegal as
any immediate and resolute attack would have
been?

We are known to harbor no unfriendly feeling
toward Hungary. We stood by her during the
struggles; we may be allowed to say that our paper, the *Neue Rheinische Zeitung,* * has done
more than any other to render the Hungarian
cause popular in Germany, by explaining the na-

---

*) "Die Neue Rheinische Zeitung" (The New
Rhenish Gazette). After the March revolution, 1848,
Marx returned from Paris to Germany, and settling down—for the time being—at Cologne, founded this paper. Although the "Neue Rheinische Zeitung" never went in for propounding "Communist
schemes," as Mr. Dawson, e. g., says it did, it became a very nightmare to the Government. Reac-
tionaries and Liberals alike denounced the "Gazette," especially after Marx's brilliant defence of the
Paris Insurrection of June. The state of siege being declared in Cologne, the "Gazette" was sus-
pended for six weeks—only to appear with a bigger
reputation and bigger circulation than before. After
the Prussian "coup d'état" in November, the "Gazette" published at the head of every issue an appeal to the people to refuse to pay taxes, and to
meet force by force. For this and certain other
articles the paper was twice prosecuted. On the first
occasion the accused were Marx, Engels, and Korff;
on the second and more important trial, they were
Marx, Schapper, and Schneider. The accused were
charged with "inciting the people to armed resistance against the Government and its officials."
Marx mainly conducted the defence, and delivered
a brilliant speech. "Marx refrains" (in this speech)
"from all oratorical flourish; he goes straight to the

ture of the struggle between the Magyar and
Slavonian races, and by following up the Hungarian war in a series of articles which have had
paid them the compliment of being plagiarized
in almost every subsequent book upon the subject, the works of native Hungarians and "eye-
witnesses" not excepted. We even now, in any
future continental convulsion, consider Hungary
as the necessary and natural ally of Germany.
But we have been severe enough upon our own

---

point, and without any peroration ends with a sum-
mary of the political situation. Anyone would think
that Marx's own personality was to deliver a political lecture to the jury. And, in fact, at the end of
the trial, one of the jurors went to Marx to thank
him, in the name of his colleagues, for the instructive lecture he had given them." (See Bernstein's
work, "Ferdinand Lassalle.") The accused were unan-
imously acquitted by the jury. Among the better
known of the contributors of the "New Rhenish
Gazette," edited by Marx, were Engels, W. Wolff,
Werth, Lassalle; while Freiligrath wrote for it his
splendid revolutionary poems. Perhaps one of the
grandest of these is the celebrated "Farewell of the
"Rhenish Gazette"," when on the 19th May, 1849,
the final number of the paper—suppressed by the
Government—appeared, printed in red type.

"When the last of crowns like glass shall break,
    On the scene our sorrows have haunted,
And the people the last dread 'Guilty' shall speak,
    By your side ye shall find me undaunted.
On Rhine or on Danube, in word and deed,
    You shall witness, true to his vow,
On the wrecks of thrones, in the midst of the freed
    The rebel who greets you now."
                    (Translated by Ernest Jones.)

countrymen, to have a right to speak out upon our neighbors; and then we have here to record facts with historical impartiality, and we must say that in this particular instance, the generous bravery of the people of Vienna was not only far more noble, but also more far-sighted than the cautious circumspection of the Hungarian Government. And, as a German, we may further be allowed to say, that not for all the showy victories and glorious battles of the Hungarian campaign, would we exchange that spontaneous, single-handed rising, and heroic resistance of the people of Vienna, our countrymen, which gave Hungary the time to organize the army that could do such great things.

The second ally of Vienna was the German people. But they were everywhere engaged in the same struggle as the Viennese. Frankfort, Baden, Cologne, had just been defeated and disarmed. In Berlin and Breslau the people were at daggers-drawn with the army, and daily expected to come to blows. Thus it was in every local center of action. Everywhere questions were pending that could only be settled by the force of arms; and now it was that for the first time were severely felt the disastrous consequences of the continuation of the old dismemberment and decentralization of Germany. The different questions in every State, every province, every town, were fundamentally the same; but they were brought forward everywhere under different shapes and pretexts, and had everywhere attained different degrees of maturity,

Thus it happened that while in every locality the decisive gravity of the events at Vienna was felt, yet nowhere could an important blow be struck with any hope of bringing the Viennese succor, or making a diversion in their favor; and there remained nothing to aid them but the Parliament and Central Power of Frankfort; they were appealed to on all hands; but what did they do?

The Frankfort Parliament and the bastard child it had brought to light by incestuous intercourse with the old German Diet, the so-called Central Power, profited by the Viennese movement to show forth their utter nullity. This contemptible Assembly, as we have seen, had long since sacrificed its virginity, and young as it was, it was already turning grey-headed and experienced in all the artifices of painting and pseudo-diplomatic prostitution. Of the dreams and illusions of power, of German regeneration and unity, that in the beginning had pervaded it, nothing remained but a set of Teutonic clap-trap phraseology, that was repeated on every occasion, and a firm belief of each individual member in his own importance, as well as in the credulity of the public. The original naivety was discarded; the representatives of the German people had turned practical men, that is to say, they had made it out that the less they did, and the more they prated, the safer would be their position as the umpires of the fate of Germany. Not that they considered their proceedings superfluous; quite the contrary. But they had found out that all really great questions, being to them forbidden ground, had better be let alone, and there, like a set of Byzantine doctors of the Lower Empire, they discussed with an importance and assiduity worthy of the fate that at last overtook them, theoretical dogmas long ago settled in every part of the civilized world, or microscopical practical questions which never led to any practical result. Thus, the Assembly being a sort of Lancastrian School for the mutual instruction of members, and being, therefore, very important to themselves, they were persuaded it was doing even more than the German people had a right to expect, and looked upon everyone as a traitor to the country who had impudence to ask them to come to any result.

When the Viennese insurrection broke out, there was a host of interpellations, debates, motions, and amendments upon it, which, of course, led to nothing. The Central Power was to interfere. It sent two commissioners, Welcker, the ex-Liberal, and Mosle, to Vienna. The travels of Don Quixote and Sancho Panza form matter for an Odyssey in comparison with the heroic feats and wonderful adventures of those two knight-errants of German Unity. Not daring to go to Vienna, they were bullied by Windischgrätz, wondered at by the idiot Emperor, and impudently hoaxed by the Minister Stadion. Their despatches and reports are perhaps the only portion of the Frankfort transactions that will retain a place in German literature; they are a perfect satirical romance, ready cut and dried, and

an eternal monument of disgrace for the Frankfort Assembly and its Government.

The left side of the Assembly had also sent
two commissioners to Vienna, in order to uphold
its authority there—Froebel and Robert Blum.
Blum, when danger drew near, judged rightly
that here the great battle of the German Revolution was to be fought, and unhesitatingly resolved to stake his head on the issue. Froebel,
on the contrary, was of opinion that it was his
duty to preserve himself for the important duties
of his post at Frankfort. Blum was considered
one of the most eloquent men of the Frankfort
Assembly; he certainly was the most popular.
His eloquence would not have stood the test of
any experienced Parliamentary Assembly; he
was too fond of the shallow declamations of a
German dissenting preacher, and his arguments
wanted both philosophical acumen and acquaint-
ance with practical matters of fact. In politics
he belonged to "Moderate Democracy," a rather
indefinite sort of thing, cherished on account of
this very want of definiteness in its principles.
But with all this Robert Blum was by nature a
thorough, though somewhat polished, plebeian,
and in decisive moments his plebeian instinct and
plebeian energy got the better of his indefinite-
ness, and, therefore, indecisive political persua-
sion and knowledge. In such moments he raised
himself far above the usual standard of his cap-
acities.

Thus, in Vienna, he saw at a glance that here,
not in the midst of the would-be elegant debates

of Frankfort, the fate of his country would have to be decided. He at once made up his mind, gave up all idea of retreat, took a command in the revolutionary force, and behaved with extraordinary coolness and decision. It was he who retarded for a considerable time the taking of the town, and covered one of its sides from attack by burning the Tabor Bridge over the Danube. Everybody knows how, after the storming, he was arrested, tried by court-martial, and shot. He died like a hero. And the Frankfort Assembly, horrorstruck as it was, yet took the bloody insult with a seeming good grace. A resolution was carried, which, by the softness and diplomatic decency of its language, was more an insult to the grave of the murdered martyr than a damning stain upon Austria. But it was not to be expected that this contemptible Assembly should resent the assassination of one of its members, particularly of the leader of the Left.

LONDON, March, 1852.

XIII.

THE PRUSSIAN ASSEMBLY—THE NATIONAL ASSEMBLY.

APRIL 17th, 1852.

ON the 1st of November Vienna fell, and on the 9th of the same month the dissolution of the Constituent Assembly in Berlin showed how much this event had at once raised the spirit and the strength of the Counter-Revolutionary party all over Germany.

The events of the summer of 1848 in Prussia are soon told. The Constituent Assembly, or rather "the Assembly elected for the purpose of agreeing upon a Constitution with the Crown," and its majority of representatives of the middle class interest, had long since forfeited all public esteem by lending itself to all the intrigues of the Court, from fear of the more energetic elements of the population. They had confirmed, or rather restored, the obnoxious privileges of feudalism, and thus betrayed the liberty and the interests of the peasantry. They had neither been able to draw up a Constitution, nor to amend in any way the general legislation. They had occupied themselves almost exclusively with nice theoretical distinctions, mere formalities, and questions of constitutional etiquette. The Assembly, in fact, was more a school of Parliamentary *savoir vivre* for its members, than a body in which the people could take any interest. The majorities were, besides, very nicely balanced, and almost always decided by the wavering centers whose oscillations from right to left, and *vice versa,* upset, first the ministry of Camphausen, then that of Auerswald and Hansemann. But while thus the Liberals, here as everywhere else, let the occasion slip out of their hands, the Court reorganized its elements of strength among the nobility, and the most uncultivated portion of the rural population, as well as in the army and the bureaucracy. After Hansemann's downfall, a ministry of bureaucrats and military officers, all staunch reactionists, was formed, which, however, seemingly gave way to the demands of the Parliament; and the Assembly acting upon the commodious principle of "measures, not men," were actually duped into applauding this ministry, while they, of course, had no eyes for the concentration and organization of Counter-Revolutionary forces, which that same ministry carried on pretty openly. At last, the signal being given by the fall of Vienna, the King dismissed its ministers, and replaced them by "men of action," under the leadership of the present premier, Manteufel. Then the dreaming Assembly at once awoke to the danger; it passed a vote of no confidence in the Cabinet, which was at once re-

plied to by a decree removing the Assembly from
Berlin, where it might, in case of a conflict, count
upon the support of the masses, to Brandenburg,
a petty provincial town dependent entirely upon
the Government. The Assembly, however, declared that it could not be adjourned, removed
or dissolved, except with its own consent. In
the meantime, General Wrangle entered Berlin
at the head of some forty thousand troops. In
a meeting of the municipal magistrates and the
officers of the National Guard, it was resolved
not to offer any resistance. And now, after the
Assembly and its Constituents, the Liberal bourgeoisie, had allowed the combined reactionary
party to occupy every important position, and to
wrest from their hands almost every means of
defence, began that grand comedy of "passive
and legal resistance" which they intended to be
a glorious imitation of the example of Hampden,
and of the first efforts of the Americans in the
War of Independence. Berlin was declared in a
state of siege, and Berlin remained tranquil; the
National Guard was dissolved by the Government, and its arms were delivered up with the
greatest punctuality. The Assembly was hunted
down during a fortnight, from one place of
meeting to another, and everywhere dispersed by
the military, and the members of the Assembly
begged of the citizens to remain tranquil. At
last the Government having declared the Assembly dissolved, it passed a resolution to declare
the levying of taxes illegal, and then its members
dispersed themselves over the country to organ-

ize the refusal of taxes. But they found that they had been woefully mistaken in the choice of their means. After a few agitated weeks, followed by severe measures of the Government against the Opposition, everyone gave up the idea of refusing the taxes in order to please a defunct Assembly that had not even had the courage to defend itself.

Whether it was in the beginning of November, 1848, already too late to try armed resistance, or whether a part of the army, on finding serious opposition, would have turned over to the side of the Assembly, and thus decided the matter in its favor, is a question which may never be solved. But in revolution as in war, it is always necessary to show a strong front, and he who attacks is in the advantage; and in revolution as in war, it is of the highest necessity to stake everything on the decisive moment, whatever the odds may be. There is not a single successful revolution in history that does not prove the truth of these axioms. Now, for the Prussian Revolution, the decisive moment had come in November, 1848; the Assembly, at the head, officially, of the whole revolutionary interest, did neither show a strong front, for it receded at every advance of the enemy; much less did it attack, for it chose even not to defend itself; and when the decisive moment came, when Wrangle, at the head of forty thousand men, knocked at the gates of Berlin, instead of finding, as he and all his officers fully expected, every street studded with barricades, every window turned into a loophole, he found the gates open, and the streets obstructed only by peaceful Berliner burghers, enjoying the joke they had played upon him, by delivering themselves up, hands and feet tied, unto the astonished soldiers. It is true, the Assembly and the people, if they had resisted, might have been beaten; Berlin might have been bombarded, and many hundreds might have been killed, without preventing the ultimate victory of the Royalist party. But that was no reason why they should surrender their arms at once. A well-contested defeat is a fact of as much revolutionary importance as an easily-won victory. The defeats of Paris in June, 1848, and of Vienna in October, certainly did far more in revolutionizing the minds of the people of these two cities than the victories of February and March. The Assembly and the people of Berlin would, probably, have shared the fate of the two towns above-named; but they would have fallen gloriously, and would have left behind themselves, in the minds of the survivors, a wish of revenge which in revolutionary times is one of the highest incentives to energetic and passionate action. It is a matter of course that, in every struggle, he who takes up the gauntlet risks being beaten; but is that a reason why he should confess himself beaten, and submit to the yoke without drawing the sword?

In a revolution he who commands a decisive position and surrenders it, instead of forcing the enemy to try his hands at an assault, invariably deserves to be treated as a traitor.

The same decree of the King of Prussia which dissolved the Constituent Assembly also proclaimed a new Constitution, founded upon the draft which had been made by a Committee of that Assembly, but enlarging in some points the powers of the Crown, and rendering doubtful in others those of the Parliament. This Constitution established two Chambers, which were to meet soon for the purpose of confirming and revising it.

We need hardly ask where the German National Assembly was during the "legal and peaceful" struggle of the Prussian Constitutionalists. It was, as usual, at Franfort, occupied with passing very tame resolutions against the proceedings of the Prussian Government, and admiring the "imposing spectacle of the passive, legal, and unanimous resistance of a whole people against brutal force." The Central Government sent commissioners to Berlin to intercede between the Ministry and the Assembly; but they met the same fate as their predecessors at Olmütz, and were politely shown out. The Left of the National Assembly, *i. e.,* the so-called Radical party, sent also their commissioners; but after having duly convinced themselves of the utter helplessness of the Berlin Assembly, and confessed their own equal helplessness, they returned to Frankfort to report progress, and to testify to the admirably peaceful conduct of the population of Berlin. Nay, more; when Herr Bassermann, one of the Central Government's commissioners, reported that the late stringent measures of the

Prussian ministers were not without foundation, inasmuch as there had of late been seen loitering about the streets of Berlin sundry, savage-looking characters, such as always appear previous to anarchical movements (and which ever since have been named "Bassermannic characters"), these worthy deputies of the Left and energetic representatives of the revolutionary interest actually arose to make oath, and testify that such was not the case! Thus within two months the total impotency of the Frankfort Assembly was signally proved. There could be no more glaring proofs that this body was totally inadequate to its task; nay, that it had not even the remotest idea of what its task really was. The fact that both in Vienna and in Berlin the fate of the Revolution was settled, that in both these capitals the most important and vital questions were disposed of, without the existence of the Frankfort Assembly ever being taken the slightest notice of—this fact alone is sufficient to establish that the body in question was a mere debating-club, composed of a set of dupes, who allowed the Governments to use them as Parliamentary puppet, shown to amuse the shopkeepers and petty tradesmen of petty States and petty towns, as long as it was considered convenient to divert the attention of these parties. How long this was considered convenient we shall soon see. But it is a fact worthy of attention that among all the "eminent" men of this Assembly there was not one who had the slightest apprehension of the part they were made to perform, and that even up to the present day ex-members of the Frankfort Club have invariably organs of historical perception quite peculiar to themselves.

LONDON, March, 1852.

XIV.

THE RESTORATION OF ORDER — DIET AND CHAMBER

APRIL 24th, 1852.

THE first months of the year 1849 were employed by the Austrian and Prussian Governments in following up the advantages obtained in October and November, 1848. The Austrian Diet, ever since the taking of Vienna, had carried on a merely nominal existence in a small Moravian country-town, named Kremsir. Here the Slavonian deputies, who, with their constituents, had been mainly instrumental in raising the Austrian Government from its prostration, were singularly punished for their teachery against the European Revolution. As soon as the Government had recovered its strength, it treated the Diet and its Slavonian majority with the utmost contempt, and when the first successes of the Imperial arms foreboded a speedy termination of the Hungarian War, the Diet, on the 4th of March, was dissolved, and the deputies dispersed by military force. Then at last the Slavonians saw that they were duped, and then they shouted:

"Let us go to Frankfort and carry on there the
opposition which we cannot pursue here!" But
it was then too late, and the very fact that they
had no other alternative than either to remain
quiet or to join the impotent Frankfort Assembly, this fact alone was sufficient to show their
utter helplessness.

Thus ended for the present, and most likely
for ever, the attempts of the Slavonians of Germany to recover an independent national existence. Scattered remnants of numerous nations,
whose nationality and political vitality had long
been extinguished, and who in consequence had
been obliged, for almost a thousand years, to
follow in the wake of a mightier nation, their
conqueror, the same as the Welsh in England,
the Basques in Spain, the Bas-Bretons in France,
and at a more recent period the Spanish and
French Creoles in those portions of North America occupied of late by the Anglo-American race
—these dying nationalities, the Bohemians, Ca-
rinthians, Dalmatians, etc., had tried to profit by
the universal confusion of 1848, in order to restore their political *status quo* of A. D. 800. The
history of a thousand years ought to have shown
them that such a retrogression was impossible;
that if all the territory east of the Elbe and Saale
had at one time been occupied by kindred Slavonians, this fact merely proved the historical tendency, and at the same time physical and intellectual power of the German nation to subdue,
absorb, and assimilate its ancient eastern neighbors; that this tendency of absorption on the

part of the Germans had always been, and still
was, one of the mightiest means by which the
civilization of Western Europe had been spread
in the east of that continent; that it could only
cease whenever the process of Germanization had
reached the frontier of large, compact, unbroken
nations, capable of an independent national life,
such as the Hungarians, and in some degree the
Poles; and that, therefore, the natural and inevitable fate of these dying nations was to allow
this process of dissolution and absorption by their
stronger neighbors to complete itself. Certainly
this is no very flattering prospect for the national ambition of the Panslavistic dreamers who
succeeded in agitating a portion of the Bohemian
and South Slavonian people; but can they expect that history would retrograde a thousand
years in order to please a few phthisical bodies
of men, who in every part of the territory they
occupy are interspersed with and surrounded by
Germans, who from time almost immemorial
have had for all purposes of civilization no other
language but the German, and who lack the very
first conditions of national existence, numbers and
compactness of territory? Thus, the Panslavistic
rising, which everywhere in the German and
Hungarian Slavonic territories was the cloak for
the restoration to independence of all these numberless petty nations, everywhere clashed with
the European revolutionary movements, and the
Slavonians, although pretending to fight for liberty, were invariably (the Democratic portion
of the Poles excented) found on the side of des-

potism and reaction. Thus it was in Germany, thus in Hungary, thus even here and there in Turkey. Traitors to the popular cause, supporters and chief props to the Austrian Government's cabal, they placed themselves in the position of outlaws in the eyes of all revolutionary nations. And although nowhere the mass of the people had a part in the petty squabbles about nationality raised by the Panslavistic leaders, for the very reason that they were too ignorant, yet it will never be forgotten that in Prague, in a half-German town, crowds of Slavonian fanatics cheered and repeated the cry: "Rather the Russian knout than German Liberty!" After their first evaporated effort in 1848, and after the lesson the Austrian Government gave them, it is not likely that another attempt at a later opportunity will be made. But if they should try again under similar pretexts to ally themselves to the counter-revolutionary force, the duty of Germany is clear. No country in a state of revolution and involved in external war can tolerate a Vendée in its very heart.

As to the Constitution proclaimed by the Emperor at the same time with the dissolution of the Diet, there is no need to revert to it, as it never had a practical existence, and is now done away with altogether. Absolutism has been restored in Austria to all intents and purposes ever since the 4th March, 1849.

In Prussia, the Chambers met in February for the ratification and revision of the new Charter proclaimed by the King. They sat for about six

weeks, humble and meek enough in their behav·
ior toward the Government, yet not quite prepared to go the lengths the King and his ministers wished them to go. Therefore, as soon as
a suitable occasion presented itself, they were
dissolved.

Thus both Austria and Prussia had for the
moment got rid of the shackles of parliamentary
control. The Governments now concentrated all
power in themselves, and could bring that power
to bear wherever is was wanted: Austria upon
Hungary and Italy, Prussia upon Germany. For
Prussia, too, was preparing for a campaign by
which "order" was to be restored in the smaller
States.

Counter-revolution being now paramount in
the two great centres of action in Germany,—in
Vienna and Berlin,—there remained only the
lesser States in which the struggle was still un-
decided, although the balance there, too, was
leaning more and more against the revolutionary interest. These smaller States, we have said,
found a common centre in the National Assembly at Frankfort. Now, this so-called National
Assembly, although its reactionist spirit had long
been evident, so much so that the very people of
Frankfort had risen in arms against it, yet its
origin was of more or less revolutionary nature;
it occupied an abnormal, revolutionary position
in January; its competence had never been defined, and it had at last come to the decision—
which, however, was never recognized by the
larges States—that its resolutions had the force

of law. Under these circumstances, and when the Constitutionalist-Monarchial party saw their positions turned by the recovering Absolutists, it is not to be wondered that the Liberal, monarchical bourgeoisie of almost the whole of Germany should place their last hopes upon the majority of this Assembly, just as the petty shopkeepers in the rest, the nucleus of the Democratic party, gathered in their growing distress around the minority of that same body, which indeed formed the last compact Parliamentary phalanx of Democracy. On the other hand, the larger Governments, and particularly the Prussian Ministry, saw more and more the incompatibility of such an irregular elective body with the restored monarchical system of Germany, and if they did not at once force its dissolution, it was only because the time had not yet come, and because Prussia hoped first to use it for the furthering of its own ambitious purposes.

In the meantime, that poor Assembly itself fell into a greater and greater confusion. Its deputations and commissaries had been treated with the utmost contempt, both in Vienna and Berlin; one of its members, in spite of his parliamentary inviolability, had been executed in Vienna as a common rebel. Its decrees were nowhere heeded; if they were noticed at all by the larger powers, it was merely by protesting notes which disputed the authority of the Assembly to pass laws and resolutions binding upon their Governments. The Representative of the Assembly, the Central Executive power, was involved in diplomatic squab-

bles with almost all the Cabinets of Germany,
and, in spite of all their efforts, neither Assembly nor Central Government could bring Austria
and Prussia to state their ultimate views, plans
and demands. The Assembly, at last, commenced
to see clearly, at least so far, that it had allowed
all power to slip out of its hands, that it was at
the mercy of Austria and Prussia, and that if it
intended making a Federal Constitution for Germany at all, it must set about the thing at once
and in good earnest. And many of the valcillat-
ing members also saw clearly that they had been
egregiously duped by the Governments. But
what were they, in their impotent position, able
to do now? The only thing that could have saved
them would have been promptly and decidedly
to pass over into the popular camp; but the success, even of that step, was more than doubtful;
and then, where in this helpless crowd of unde-
cided, shortsighted, self-conceited beings, who,
when the eternal noise of contradictory rumors
and diplomatic notes completely stunned them,
sought their only consolation and support in the
everlastingly repeated assurance that they were
the best, the greatest, the wisest men of the country, and that they alone could save Germany—
where, we say, among these poor creatures, whom
a single year of Parliamentary life had turned
into complete idiots, where were the men for a
prompt and decisive resolution, much less for
energetic and consistent action?

At last the Austrian Government threw off the
mask. In its Constitution of the 4th of March,

it proclaimed Austria an indivisible monarchy, with common finances, system of customs-duties, of military establishments, thereby effacing every barrier and distinction between the German and non-German provinces. This declaration was made in the face of resolutions and articles of the intended Federal Constitution which had been already passed by the Frankfort Assembly. It was the gauntlet of war thrown down to it by Austria, and the poor Assembly had no other choice but to take it up. This it did with a deal of blustering, which Austria, in the consciousness of her power, and of the utter nothingness of the Assembly, could well afford to allow to pass. And this precious representation, as it styled itself, of the German people, in order to revenge itself for this insult on the part of Austria, saw nothing better before it than to throw itself, hands and feet tied, at the feet of the Prussian Government. Incredible as it would seem, it bent its knees before the very ministers whom it had condemned as unconstitutional and anti-popular, and whose dismissal it had in vain insisted upon. The details of this disgraceful transaction, and the tragicomical events that followed, will form the subject of our next.

LONDON, April, 1852.

XV.

THE TRIUMPH OF PRUSSIA.

JULY 27th, 1852.

WE now come to the last chapter in the history of the German Revolution; the conflict of the National Assembly with the Governments of the different States, especially of Prussia; the insurrection of Southern and Western Germany, and its final overthrow by Prussia.

We have already seen the Frankfort National Assembly at work. We have seen it kicked by Austria, insulted by Prussia, disobeyed by the lesser States, duped by its own impotent Central "Government," which again was the dupe of all and every prince in the country. But at last things began to look threatening for this weak, vacillating, insipid legislative body. It was forced to come to the conclusion that "the sublime idea of Germany unity was threatened in its realization," which meant neither more nor less than that the Frankfort Assembly, and all it had done, and was about to do, were very likely to end in smoke. Thus it set to work in good earnest in order to bring forth, as soon as possible, its grand

144

production, the "Imperial Constitution." There was, however, one difficulty. What Executive Government was there to be? An Executive Council? No; that would have been, they thought in their wisdom, making Germany a Republic. A "president"? That would come to the same. Thus they must revive the old Imperial dignity. But—as, of course, a prince was to be emperor —who should it be? Certainly none of the *Dii minorum gentium,* from Reuss-Schleitz-Greitz-Lobenstein-Ebersdorf up to Bavaria; neither Austria nor Prussia would have borne that. It could only be Austria or Prussia. But which of the two? There is no doubt that, under otherwise favorable circumstances, this august Assembly would be sitting up to the present day, discussing this important dilemma without being able to come to a conclusion, if the Austrian Government had not cut the Gordian knot, and saved them the trouble.

Austria knew very well that from the moment in which she could again appear before Europe with all her provinces subdued, as a strong and great European power, the very law of political gravitation would draw the remainder of Germany into her orbit, without the help of any authority which an Imperial crown, conferred by the Frankfort Assembly, could give her. Austria had been far stronger, far freer in her movements, since she shook off the powerless *crown* of the German Empire—a crown which clogged her own independent policy, while it added not one iota to her strength, either within or without

Germany. And supposing the case that Austria could not maintain her footing in Italy and Hungary, why, then she was dissolved, annihilated in Germany too, and could never pretend to re-seize a crown which had slipped from her hands while she was in the full possession of her strength. Thus Austria at once declared against all imperialist resurrections, and plainly demanded the restoration of the German Diet, the only Central Government of Germany known and recognized by the treaties of 1815; and on the 4th of March, 1849, issued that Constitution which had no other meaning than to declare Austria an indivisible, centralized, and independent monarchy, distinct even from that Germany which the Frankfort Assembly was to reorganize.

This open declaration of war left, indeed, the Frankfort wiseacres no other choice but to exclude Austria from Germany, and to create out of the remainder of that country a sort of lower empire, a "little Germany," the rather shabby Imperial mantle of which was to fall on the shoulders of His Majesty of Prussia. This, it will be recollected, was the renewal of an old project fostered already some six or eight years ago by a party of South and Middle German Liberal *doctrinaires*, who considered as a godsend the degrading circumstances by which their old crotchet was now again brought forward as the latest "new move" for the salvation of the country.

They accordingly finished, in February and March, 1849, the debate on the Imperial Consti-

tution, together with the Declaration of Rights
and the Imperial Electoral Law; not, however,
without being obliged to make, in a great many
points, the most contradictory concessions—now
to the Conservative or rather Reactionary party
—now to the more advanced factions of the Assembly. In fact, it was evident that the leadership of the Assembly, which had formerly belonged to the Right and Right Centre (the Conservatives and Reactionists), was gradually, although slowly, passing toward the Left or
Democratic side of that body. The rather dubious
position of the Austrian deputies in an Assembly
which had excluded their country from Germany, and in which they yet were called upon to
sit and vote, favored the derangement of its
equipoise; and thus, as early as the end of February, the Left Centre and Left found themselves, by the help of the Austrian votes, very
generally in a majority, while on other days the
Conservative faction of the Austrians, all of a
sudden, and for the fun of the thing, voting with
the Right, threw the balance again on the other
side. They intended, by these sudden *soubresauts,*
to bring the Assembly into contempt, which, however, was quite unnecessary, the mass of the people being long since convinced of the utter hol-
lowness and futility of anything coming from
Frankfort. What a specimen of a Constitution,
in the meantime, was framed under such jump-
ing and counter-jumping, may easily be imagined.

The Left of the Assembly—this *élite* and pride

of revolutionary Germany, as it believed itself
to be—was entirely intoxicated with the few
paltry successes it obtained by the good-will, or
rather the ill-will, of a set of Austrian politicians, acting under the instigation and for the interest of Austrian despotism. Whenever the
slightest approximation to their own not very
well-defined principles had, in a homœopathi-
cally diluted shape, obtained a sort of sanction
by the Frankfort Assembly, these Democrats
proclaimed that they had saved the country and
the people. These poor, weak-minded men, during the course of their generally very obscure
lives, had been so little accustomed to anything
like success, that they actually believed their
paltry amendments, passed with two or three
votes majority, would change the face of Europe.
They had, from the beginning of their legislative
career, been more imbued than any other faction
of the Assembly with that incurable malady
Parliamentary crétinism, a disorder which pene-
trates its unfortunate victims with the solemn
conviction that the whole world, its history and
future, are governed and determined by a majority of votes in that particular representative
body which has the honor to count them among
its members, and that all and everything going
on outside the walls of their house—wars, revolutions, railway-constructing, colonizing of whole
new continents, California gold discoveries, Central American canals, Russian armies, and whatever else may have some little claim to influence
upon the destinies of mankind—is nothing com-

pared with the incommensurable events hinging
upon the important question, whatever it may
be, just at that moment occupying the attention
of their honorable house. Thus it was the Democratic party of the Assembly, by effectually
smuggling a few of their nostrums into the "Imperial Constitution," first became bound to support it, although in every essential point it flatly
contradicted their own oft-proclaimed principles,
and at last, when this mongrel work was abandoned, and bequeathed to them by its main authors, accepted the inheritance, and held out for
this *Monarchical* Constitution, even in opposition
to everybody who *then* proclaimed their own *Republican* principles.

But it must be confessed that in this the contradiction was merely apparent. The indetermi-
nate, self-contradictory, immature character of
the Imperial Constitution was the very image of
the immature, confused, conflicting political ideas
of these Democratic gentlemen. And if their own
sayings and writings—as far as they could write
—were not sufficient proof of this, their actions
would furnish such proof; for among sensible
people it is a matter of course to judge of a man,
not by his professions, but his actions; not by
what he pretends to be, but by what he does,
and what he really is; and the deeds of these
heroes of German Democracy speak loud enough
for themselves, as we shall learn by and by. However, the Imperial Constitution, with all its ap-
pendages and paraphernalia, was definitely passed, and on the 28th of March, the King of Prus-

sia was, by 290 votes against 248 who abstained, and 200 who were absent, elected Emperor of Germany *minus Austria*. The historical irony was complete; the Imperial farce executed in the streets of astonished Berlin, three days after the Revolution of March 18th, 1848, by Frederick William IV., while in a state which elsewhere would come under the Maine Liquor Law—this disgusting farce, just one year afterwards, had been sanctioned by the pretended Representative Assembly of all Germany. That, then, was the result of the German Revolution!

LONDON, July, 1852.

XVI.

THE ASSEMBLY AND THE GOVERN-
MENTS.

AUGUST 19th, 1852.

THE National Assembly of Frankfort, after having elected the King of Prussia Emperor of Germany (*minus* Austria), sent a deputation to Berlin to offer him the crown, and then adjourned. On the 3rd of April, Frederick William received the deputies. He told them that, although he accepted the right of precedence over all the other princes of Germany, which this vote of the people's representatives had given him, yet he could not accept the Imperial crown as long as he was not sure that the remaining princes acknowledged his supremacy, and the Imperial Constitution conferring those rights upon him. It would be, he added, for the Governments of Germany to see whether this Constitution was such as could be ratified by them. At all events, Emperor or not, he always would be found ready, he concluded, to draw the sword against either the external or the internal foe. We shall see how he kept his promise in a manner rather startling for the National Assembly.

The Frankfort wiseacres, after profound diplomatic inquiry, at last came to the conclusion that this answer amounted to a refusal of the crown. They then (April 12th) resolved: That the Imperial Constitution was the law of the land, and must be maintained; and not seeing their way at all before them, elected a Committee of thirty, to make proposals as to the means how this Constitution could be carried out.

This resolution was the signal for the conflict between the Frankfort Assembly and the German Governments which now broke out. The middle classes, and especially the smaller trading class, had all at once declared for the new Frankfort Constitution. They could not wait any longer the moment which was "to close the Revolution." In Austria and Prussia the Revolution had, for the moment, been closed by the interference of the armed power. The classes in question would have preferred a less forcible mode of performing that operation, but they had not had a chance; the thing was done, and they had to make the best of it, a resolution which they at once took and carried out most heroically. In the smaller States, where things had been going on comparatively smoothly, the middle classes had long since been thrown back into that showy, but resultless, because powerless, parliamentary agitation, which was most congenial to themselves. The different States of Germany, as regarded each of them separately, appeared thus to have attained that new and definite form which was supposed to enable them to enter henceforth the

path of peaceful constitutional development.
There only remained one open question, that of
the new political organization of the German Con-
federacy. And this question, the only one which
still appeared fraught with danger, it was considered a necessity to resolve at once. Hence the
pressure exerted upon the Frankfort Assembly
by the middle classes, in order to induce it to
get the Constitution ready as soon as possible;
hence the resolution among the higher and lower
bourgeoisie to accept and support this Constitution, whatever it might be, in order to create a
settled state of things without delay. Thus from
the very beginning the agitation for the Imperial
Constitution arose out of a reactionary feeling,
and sprang up among these classes which were
long since tired of the Revolution.

But there was another feature in it. The first
and fundamental principles of the future German Constitution had been voted during the first
months of spring and summer, 1848, a time when
popular agitation was still rife. The resolutions
then passed, though completely reactionary *then,*
now, after the arbitrary acts of the Austrian and
Prussian Governments, appeared exceedingly
Liberal, and even Democratic. The standard of
comparison had changed. The Frankfort Assembly could not, without moral suicide, strike
out these once-voted provisions, and model the
Imperial Constitution upon those which the Austrian and Prussian Governments had dictated,
sword in hand. Besides, as we have seen, the
majority in that Assembly had changed sides,

and the Liberal and Democratic party were rising in influence. Thus the Imperial Constitution not only was distinguished by its apparently
exclusive popular origin, but at the same time,
full of contradiction as it was, it yet was the
most Liberal Constitution in all Germany. Its
greatest fault was, that it was a mere sheet of
paper, with no power to back its provisions.

Under these circumstances it was natural that
the so-called Democratic party, that is, the mass
of the petty trading class, should cling to the Imperial Constitution. This class had always been
more forward in its demands than the Liberal-
Monarchico-Constitutional bourgeoisie; it had
shown a bolder front, it had very often threatened armed resistance, it was lavish in its promises to sacrifice its blood and its existence in the
struggle for freedom; but it had already given
plenty of proofs that on the day of danger it was
nowhere, and that it never felt more comfortable
than the day after a decisive defeat, when everything being lost, it had at least the consolation
to know that somehow or other the matter *was*
settled. While, therefore, the adhesion of the
large bankers, manufacturers, and merchants was
of a more reserved character, more like a simple
demonstration in favor of the Frankfort Constitution, the class just beneath them, our valiant
Democratic shopkeepers, came forward in grand
style, and, as usual, proclaimed they would rather
spill their last drop of blood than let the Imperial Constitution fall to the ground.

Supported by these two parties, the bourgeois adherents of the Constitutional Royalty, and the more or less Democratic shopkeepers, the agitation for the immediate establishment of the Imperial Constitution gained ground rapidly, and found its most powerful expression in the Parliaments of the several States. The Chambers of Prussia, of Hanover, of Saxony, of Baden, of Wurtemberg, declared in its favor. The struggle between the Governments and the Frankfort Assembly assumed a threatening aspect.

The Governments, however, acted rapidly. The Prussian Chambers were dissolved, anti-constitutionally, as they had to revise and confirm the Constitution; riots broke out at Berlin, provoked intentionally by the Government,, and the next day, the 28th of April, the Prussian Ministry issued a circular note, in which the Imperial Constitution was held up as a most anarchical and revolutionary document, which it was for the Governments of Germany to remodel and purify. Thus Prussia denied, point-blank, that sovereign constituent power which the wise men at Frankfort had always boasted of, but never established. Thus a Congress of Princes, a renewal of the old Federal Diet, was called upon to sit in judgment on that Constitution which had already been promulgated as law. And at the same time Prussia concentrated troops at Kreuznach, three days' march from Frankfort, and called upon the smaller States to follow its example, by also dissolving their Chambers as soon as they should give their adhesion to the Frankfort Assembly. This example was speedily followed by Hanover and Saxony.

It was evident that a decision of the struggle by force of arms could not be avoided. The hostility of the Governments, the agitation among the people, were daily showing themselves in stronger colors. The military were everywhere worked upon by the Democratic citizens, and in the south of Germany with great success. Large mass meetings were everywhere held, passing resolutions to support the Imperial Constitution and the National Assembly, if need should be, with force of arms. At Cologne, a meeting of deputies of all the municipal councils of Rhenish Prussia took place for the same purpose. In the Palatinate, at Bergen, Fulda, Nuremberg, in the Odenwald, the peasantry met by myriads and worked themselves up into enthusiasm. At the same time the Constituent Assembly of France dissolved, and the new elections were prepared amid violent agitation, while on the eastern frontier of Germany, the Hungarians had within a month, by a succession of brilliant victories, rolled back the tide of Austrian invasion from the Theiss to the Leitha, and were every day expected to take Vienna by storm. Thus, popular imagination being on all hands worked up to the highest pitch, and the aggressive policy of the Governments defining itself more clearly every day, a violent collision could not be avoided, and cowardly imbecility only could persuade itself that the struggle was to come off peaceably. But this cowardly imbecility was most extensively represented in the Frankfort Assembly.

LONDON, July, 1852.

XVII.

INSURRECTION.

THE inevitable conflict between the National Assembly of Frankfort and the States Governments of Germany at last broke out in open hostilities during the first days of May, 1849. The Austrian deputies, recalled by their Government, had already left the Assembly and returned home, with the exception of a few members of the Left or Democratic party. The great body of the Conservative members, aware of the turn things were about to take, withdrew even before they were called upon to do so by their respective Governments. Thus, even independently of the causes which in the foregoing letters have been shown to strengthen the influence of the Left, the mere desertion of their posts by the members of the Right, sufficed to turn the old minority into a majority of the Assembly. The new majority, which, at no former time, had dreamed of ever obtaining that good fortune, had profited by their places on the opposition benches to spout against the weakness, the indecision, the indolence of the old majority, and of its Imperial Lieutenancy. Now all at once, *they* were called on to replace that old majority. *They* were now to show what they could perform. Of course, *their* career was to be one of energy, determination, activity. *They,* the *élite* of Germany, would soon be able to drive onwards the senile Lieutenant of the Empire, and his vacillating ministers, and in case that was impossible they would — there could be no doubt about it — by force of the sovereign right of the people, depose that impotent Government, and replace it by an energetic, indefatigable Executive, who would assure the salvation of Germany. Poor fellows! *Their* rule — if rule it can be named, where no one obeyed — was a still more ridiculous affair than even the rule of their predecessors.

The new majority declared that, in spite of all obstacles, the Imperial Constitution must be carried out, and *at once;* that on the 15th of July ensuing, the people were to elect the deputies of the new House of Representatives, and that this House was to meet at Frankfort on the 15th of August following. Now, this was an open declaration of war against those Governments that had not recognized the Imperial Constitution, the foremost among which were Prussia, Austria, Bavaria, comprising more than three-fourths of the German population; a declaration of war which was speedily accepted by them. Prussia and Bavaria, too, recalled the deputies sent from their territories to Frankfort, and hastened their military preparations against the National Assembly, while, on the other hand, the demonstrations of the Democratic party (out of Parliament) in favor of the Imperial Constitution and of the National Assembly, acquired a more turbulent and violent character, and the mass of the working people, led by the men of the most extreme party, were ready to take up arms in a cause which, if it was not their own, at least gave them a chance of somewhat approaching their aims by clearing Germany of its old monarchical encumbrances. Thus everywhere the people and the Governments were at daggers drawn upon this subject; the outbreak was inevitable; the mine was charged, and it only wanted a spark to make it explode. The dissolution of the Chambers in Saxony, the calling in of the Landwehr (military reserve)) in Prussia, the open resistance of the Government to the Imperial Constitution, were such sparks; they fell, and all at once the country was in a blaze. In Dresden, on the 4th of May, the people victoriously took possession of the town, and drove out the King, while all the surrounding districts sent re-inforcements to the insurgents. In Rhenish Prussia and Westphalia the Landwehr refused to march, took possession of the arsenals, and armed itself in defence of the Imperial Constitution. In the Palatinate the people seized the Bavarian Government officials, and the public moneys, and instituted a Committee of Defence, which placed the province under the protection of the National Assembly. In Würtemberg the people forced the King to acknowledge the Imperial Constitution, and in Baden the army, united with the people, forced the Grand Duke to flight, and erected a Provincial Government. In other parts of Germany the people only awaited a decisive signal from the National Assembly to rise in arms and place themselves at its disposal.

The position of the National Assembly was far more favorable than could have been expected after its ignoble career. The western half of Germany had taken up arms in its behalf; the military everywhere were vacillating; in the lesser States they were undoubtedly favorable to the movement. Austria was prostrated by the victorious advance of the Hungarians, and Russia, that reserve force of the German Governments, was straining all its powers in order to support Austria against the Magyar armies. There was only Prussia to subdue, and with the revolutionary sympathies existing in that country, a chance certainly existed of attaining that end. Everything then depended upon the conduct of the Assembly.

Now, insurrection is an art quite as much as war or any other, and subject to certain rules of proceeding, which, when neglected, will produce the ruin of the party neglecting them. Those rules, logical deductions from the nature of the parties and the circumstances one has to deal with in such a case, are so plain and simple that the short experience of 1848 had made the Germans pretty well acquainted with them. Firstly, never play with insurrection unless you are fully prepared to face the consequences of your play. Insurrection is a calculus with very indefinite magnitudes, the value of which may change every day; the forces opposed to you have all the advantage of organization, discipline, and habitual authority; unless you bring strong odds against them you are defeated and ruined. Secondly, the insurrectionary career once entered upon, act with the greatest determination, and on the offensive. The defensive is the death of every armed rising; it is lost before it measures itself with its enemies. Surprise your antagonists while their forces are scattering, prepare new successes, however small, but daily; keep up the moral ascendancy which the first successful rising has given to you; rally those vacillating elements to your side which always follow the strongest impulse, and which always look out for the safer side; force your enemies to a retreat before they can collect their strength against you; in the words of Danton, the greatest master of revolutionary policy yet known, *de l'audace, de l'audace, encore de l'audace!*

What, then, was the National Assembly of Frankfort to do if it would escape the certain ruin which it was threatened with? First of all, to see clearly through the situation, and to convince itself that there was now no other choice than either to submit to the Governments unconditionally, or take up the cause of the armed insurrection without reserve or hesitation. Secondly, to publicly recognize all the insurrections that had already broken out, and to call the people to take up arms everywhere in defence of the national representation, outlawing all princes, ministers and others who should dare to oppose the sovereign people represented by its mandatories. Thirdly, to at once depose the German Imperial Lieutenant, to create a strong, active, unscrupulous Executive, to call insurgent troops to Frankfort for its immediate protection, thus offering at the same time a legal pretext for the spread of the insurrection, to organize into a compact body all the forces at its disposal, and, in short, to profit quickly and unhesitatingly by every available means for strengthening its position and impairing that of its opponents.

Of all this the virtuous Democrats in the Frankfort Assembly did just the contrary. Not content with letting things take the course they liked, these worthies went so far as to suppress by their opposition all insurrectionary movements which were preparing. Thus, for instance, did Herr Karl Vogt at Nuremberg. They allowed the insurrections of Saxony, of Rhenish Prussia, of Westphalia to be suppressed without any other help than a posthumous, sentimental protest against the unfeeling violence of the Prussian Government. They kept up an underhand diplomatic intercourse with the South German insurrections but never gave them the support of their open acknowledgment. They knew that the Lieutenant of the Empire sided with the Governments, and yet they called upon *him*, who never stirred, to oppose the intrigues of these Governments. The ministers of the Empire, old

Conservatives, ridiculed this impotent Assembly in every sitting, and they suffered it. And when William Wolff, * a Silesian deputy, and one of the editors of the *New Rhenish Gazette,* called upon them to outlaw the Lieutenant of the Empire — who was, he justly said, nothing but the first and greatest traitor to the Empire, he was hooted down by the unanimous and virtuous indignation of those Democratic Revolutionists! In short, they went on talking, protesting, proclaiming, pronouncing, but never had the courage or the sense to act; while the hostile troops of the Governments drew nearer and nearer, and their own Executive, the Lieutenant of the Empire, was busily plotting with the German princes their speedy destruction. Thus even the last vestige of consideration was lost to this contemptible Assembly; the insurgents who had

---

*) The "Wolff" here alluded to is Wilhelm Wolff, the beloved friend of Marx and Engels, who—to distinguish him from the many other "Wolffs" in the movement at this period—was known to his intimates as "Lupus." It is to this Silesion peasant that Marx dedicated the first volume of "Capital."

"Dedicated
To My Never-To-Be-Forgotten Friend
The Brave, True, Noble Fighter In The Van-Guard
Of The Proletariat,
WILHELM WOLFF.

Born at Tornau, June 21st, 1809. Died in exile at Manchester, 9th May, 1864."

risen to defend it ceased to care any more for it, and when at last it came to a shameful end, as we shall see, it died without anybody taking any notice of its unhonored exit.

LONDON, August, 1852.

XVIII.

PETTY TRADERS.

OCTOBER 2, 1852.

IN our last we showed that the struggle between the German Governments on the one side,
and the Frankfort Parliament on the other, had
ultimately acquired such a degree of violence
that in the first days of May, a great portion of
Germany broke out in open insurrection; first
Dresden, then the Bavarian Palatinate, parts of
Rhenish Prussia, and at last Baden.

In all cases, the *real fighting* body of the insurgents, that body which first took up arms and
gave battle to the troops consisted of the *working classes of the towns*. A portion of the poorer
country population, laborers and petty farmers,
generally joined them after the outbreak of the
conflict. The greater number of the young men
of all classes, below the capitalist class, were to
be found, for a time at least, in the ranks of the
insurgent armies, but this rather indiscriminate
aggregate of young men very soon thinned as
the aspect of affairs took a somewhat serious
turn. The students particularly, those "representatives of intellect," as they liked to call them-

selves, were the first to quit their standards, unless they were retained by the bestowal of officer's rank, for which they, of course, had very seldom any qualifications.

The working class entered upon this insurrection as they would have done upon any other which promised either to remove some obstacles in their progress towards political dominion and social revolution, or, at least, to tie the more influential but less courageous classes of society to a more decided and revolutionary course than they had followed hitherto. The working class took up arms with a full knowledge that this was, in the direct bearings of the case, no quarrel of its own; but it followed up its only true policy, to allow no class that has risen on its shoulders (as the bourgeoisie had done in 1848) to fortify its class-government, without opening, at least, a fair field to the working classes for the struggle for its own interests, and, in any case, to bring matters to a crisis, by which either the nation was fairly and irresistibly launched in the revolutionary career, or else the *status quo* before the Revolution restored as nearly as possible, and, thereby, a new revolution rendered unavoidable. In both cases the working classes represented the real and well-understood interest of the nation at large, in hastening as much as possible that revolutionary course which for the old societies of civilized Europe has now become a historical necessity, before any of them can again aspire to a more quiet and regular development of their resources.

As to country people that joined the insurrection, they were principally thrown into the arms of the Revolutionary party, partly by the relatively enormous load of taxation, and partly of feudal burdens pressing upon them.

Without any initiative of their own, they formed the tail of the other classes engaged in the insurrection, wavering between the working men on the one side, and the petty trading class on the other. Their own private social position, in almost every case, decided which way they turned; the agricultural laborer generally supported the city artisan; the small farmer was apt to go hand in hand with the small shopkeeper.

This class of petty tradesmen, the great importance and influence of which we have already several times adverted to, may be considered as the leading class of the insurrection of May, 1849. There being, this time, none of the large towns of Germany among the center of the movement, the petty trading class, which in middling and lesser towns always predominates, found the means of getting the direction of the movement into its hands. We have, moreover, seen that, in this struggle for the Imperial Constitution, and for the rights of the German Parliament, there were the interests of this peculiar class at stake. The Provisional Governments formed in all the insurgent districts represented in the majority of each of them this section of the people, and the length they went to may therefore be fairly taken as the measure of what the German petty bourgeoisie is capable of —

capable, as we shall see, of nothing but ruining
any movement that entrusts itself to its hands.

The petty bourgeoisie, great in boasting, is
very impotent for action, and very shy in risking
anything. The *mesquin* character of its commercial transactions and its credit operations is emi-
nently apt to stamp its character with a want of
energy and enterprise; it is, then, to be expected
that similar qualities will mark its political career. Accordingly the petty bourgeoisie encour-
aged insurrection by big words, and great boasting as to what it was going to do; it was eager
to seize upon power as soon as the insurrection,
much against its will, had broken out; it used
this power to no other purpose but to destroy the
effects of the insurrection. Wherever an armed
conflict had brought matters to a serious crisis,
there the shopkeepers stood aghast at the dangerous situation created for them; aghast at the people who had taken their boasting appeals to arms
in earnest; aghast at the power thus thrust into
their own hands; aghast, above all, at the consequences for themselves, for their social positions, for their fortunes, of the policy in which
they were forced to engage themselves. Were
they not expected to risk "life and property," as
they used to say, for the cause of the insurrection? Were they not forced to take official positions in the insurrection, whereby, in the case of
defeat, they risked the loss of their capital? And
in case of victory, were they not sure to be immediately turned out of office, and to see their
entire policy subverted by the victorious prole-

tarians who formed the main body of their fighting army? Thus placed between opposing dangers which surrounded them on every side, the petty bourgeoisie knew not to turn its power to any other account than to let everything take its chance, whereby, of course, there was lost what little chance of success there might have been, and thus to ruin the insurrection altogether. Its policy, or rather want of policy, everywhere was the same, and, therefore, the insurrections of May, 1849, in all parts of Germany, are all cut out to the same pattern.

In Dresden, the struggle was kept on for four days in the streets of the town. The shopkeepers of Dresden, the "communal guard," not only did not fight, but in many instances favored the proceedings of the troops against the insurgents. These again consisted almost exclusively of working men from the surrounding manufacturing districts. They found an able and cool-headed commander in the Russian refugee Michael Bakunin, who afterwards was taken prisoner, and now is confined in the dungeons of Munkacs, Hungary. The intervention of numerous Prussian troops crushed this insurrection.

In Rhenish Prussia the actual fighting was of little importance. All the large towns being fortresses commanded by citadels, there could be only skirmishing on the part of the insurgents. As soon as a sufficient number of troops had been drawn together, there was an end to armed opposition.

In the Palatinate and Baden, on the contrary,

a rich, fruitful province and an entire state fell into the hands of the insurrection. Money, arms, soldiers, warlike stores, everything was ready for use. The soldiers of the regular army themselves joined the insurgents; nay, in Baden, they were amongst the foremost of them. The insurrections in Saxony and Rhenish Prussia sacrificed themselves in order to gain time for the organization of the South German movement. Never was there such a favorable position for a provincial and partial insurrection as this. A revolution was expected in Paris; the Hungarians were at the gates of Vienna; in all the central States of Germany, not only the people, but even the troops, were strongly in favor of the insurrection, and only wanted an opportunity to join it openly. And yet the movement, having once got into the hands of the petty bourgeoisie, was ruined from its very beginning. The petty bourgeois rulers, particularly of Baden — Herr Brentano at the head of them — never forgot that by usurping the place and prerogatives of the "lawful" sovereign, the Grand Duke, they were committing high treason. They sat down in their ministerial armchairs with the consciousness of criminality in their hearts. What can you expect of such cowards? They not only abandoned the insurrection to its own uncentralized, and therefore ineffective, spontaneity, they actually did everything in their power to take the sting out of the movement, to unman, to destroy it. And they succeeded, thanks to the zealous support of that deep class of politicians, the "Democratic" heroes of the petty bourgeoisie, who actually thought they were "saving the country," while they allowed themselves to be led by their noses by a few men of a sharper cast, such as Brentano.

As to the fighting part of the business, never were military operations carried on in a more slovenly, more stolid way than under the Baden General-in-Chief Sigel, an ex-lieutenant of the regular army. Everything was got into confusion, every good opportunity was lost, every precious moment was loitered away with planning colossal, but impracticable projects, until, when at last the talented Pole Mieroslawski, took up the command, the army was disorganized, beaten, dispirited, badly provided for, opposed to an enemy four times more numerous, and withal, he could do nothing more than fight, at Waghäusel, a glorious though unsuccessful battle, carry out a clever retreat, offer a last hopeless fight under the walls of Rastatt, and resign. As in every insurrectionary war where armies are mixed of well-drilled, soldiers and raw levies, there was plenty of heroism, and plenty of unsoldierlike, often unconceivable panic, in the revolutionary army; but, imperfect as it could not but be, it had at least the satisfaction that four times its number were not considered sufficient to put it to the rout, and that a hundred thousand regular troops, in a campaign against twenty thousand insurgents, treated them, militarily, with as much respect as if they had to fight the Old Guard of Napoleon.

In May the insurrection had broken out; by the middle of July, 1849, it was entirely subdued, and the first German Revolution was closed.

LONDON. (Undated.)

XIX.

THE CLOSE OF THE INSURRECTION.

OCTOBER 23, 1852.

WHILE the south and west of Germany was in
open insurrection, and while it took the Governments from the first opening of hostilities at
Dresden to the capitulation of Rastatt, rather
more than ten weeks, to stifle this final blazing
up of the first German Revolution, the National
Assembly disappeared from the political theater
without any notice being taken of its exit.

We left this august body at Frankfort, per-
plexed by the insolent attacks of the Governments upon its dignity, by the impotency and
treacherous listlessness of the Central Power it
had itself created, by the risings of the petty
trading class for its defence, and of the working class for a more revolutionary ultimate end.
Desolation and despair reigned supreme among
its members; events had at once assumed such a
definite and decisive shape that in a few days the
illusions of these learned legislators as to their
real power and influence were entirely broken
down. The Conservatives, at the signal given
by the Governments, had already retired from

a body which, henceforth, could not exist any
longer, except in defiance of the constituted authorities. The Liberals gave the matter up in
utter discomfiture; they, too, threw up their com-
missions as representatives. Honorable gentlemen decamped by hundreds. From eight or nine
hundred members the number had dwindled
down so rapidly that now one hundred and fifty,
and a few days after one hundred, were declared
a quorum. And even these were difficult to mus-
ter, although the whole of the Democratic party
remained.

The course to be followed by the remnants of
a parliament was plain enough. They had only
to take their stand openly and decidedly with the
insurrection, to give it, thereby, whatever
strength legality could confer upon it, while they
themselves at once acquired an army for their
own defence. They had to summon the Central
Power to stop all hostilities at once; and if, as
could be foreseen, this power neither could nor
would do so, to depose it at once and put another more energetic Government in its place.
If insurgent troops could not be brought to
Frankfort (which, in the beginning, when the
State Governments were little prepared and still
hesitating, might have been easily done), then
the Assembly could have adjourned at once to
the very center of the insurgent district. All this
done at once, and resolutely, not later than the
middle or end of May, might have opened
chances both for the insurrection and for the
National Assembly.

But such a determined course was not to be expected from the representatives of German shopocracy. These aspiring statesmen were not at all freed from their illusions. Those members who had lost their fatal belief in the strength and inviolability of the Parliament had already taken to their heels; the Democrats who remained, were not so easily induced to give up dreams of power and greatness which they had cherished for a twelvemonth. True to the course they had hitherto pursued, they shrank back from decisive action until every chance of success, nay, every chance to succumb, with at least the honors of war, had passed away. In order, then, to develop a fictitious, busy-body sort of activity, the sheer impotency of which, coupled with its high pretension, could not but excite pity and ridicule, they continued insinuating resolutions, addresses, and requests to an Imperial Lieutenant, who not even noticed them; to ministers who were in open league with the enemy. And when at last William Wolff, member for Striegan, one of the editors of the *New Rhenish Gazette*, the only really revolutionary man in the whole Assembly, told them that if they meant what they said, they had better give over talking, and declare the Imperial Lieutenant, the chief traitor to the country, an outlaw at once; then the entire compressed virtuous indignation of these parliamentary gentlemen burst out with an energy which they never found when the Government heaped insult after insult upon them.

Of course, for Wolff's proposition was the

first sensible word spoken within the walls of St. Paul's Church; of course, for it was the very thing that was to be done, and such plain language going so direct to the purpose, could not but insult a set of sentimentalists, who were resolute in nothing but irresolution, and who, too cowardly to act, had once for all made up their minds that in doing nothing, they were doing exactly what was to be done. Every word which cleared up, like lightning, the infatuated, but intentional nebulosity of their minds, every hint that was adapted to lead them out of the labyrinth where they obstinated themselves to take up as lasting an abode as possible, every clear conception of matters as they actually stood, was, of course, a crime against the majesty of this Sovereign Assembly.

Shortly after the position of the honorable gentlemen in Frankfort became untenable, in spite of resolutions, appeals, interpellations, and proclamations, they retreated, but not into the insurgent districts; that would have been too resolute a step. They went to Stuttgart, where the Würtemberg Government kept up a sort of expectative neutrality. There, at last, they declared the Lieutenant of the Empire to have forfeited his power, and elected from their own body a Regency of five. This Regency at once proceeded to pass a Militia law, which was actually in all due force sent to all the Governments of Germany.

They, the very enemies of the Assembly, were ordered to levy forces in its defence! Then there was created — on paper, of course — an army for the defence of the National Assembly. Divisions, brigades, regiments, batteries, everything was regulated and ordained. Nothing was wanted but reality, for that army, of course, was never called into existence.

One last scheme offered itself to the General Assembly. The Democratic population from all parts of the country sent deputations to place itself at the disposal of the Parliament, and to urge it on to a decisive action. The people, knowing what the intentions of the Würtemberg Government were, implored the National Assembly to force that Government into an open and active participation with their insurgent neighbors. But no. The National Assembly, in going to Stuttgart, had delivered itself up to the tender mercies of the Würtemberg Government. The members knew it, and repressed the agitation among the people. They thus lost the last remnant of influence which they might yet have retained. They earned the contempt they deserved, and the Imperial Lieutenant put a stop to the Democratic farce by shutting up, on the 18th of June, 1849, the room where the Parliament met, and by ordering the members of the Regency to leave the country.

Next they went to Baden, into the camp of the insurrection; but there they were now useless. Nobody noticed them. The Regency, however, in the name of the Sovereign German people, continued to save the country by its exertions. It made an attempt to get recognized by foreign powers, by delivering *passports* to anybody who would accept of them. It issued proclamations, and sent commissioners to insurge those very districts of Würtemberg whose active assistance it had refused when it was yet time; of course, without effect. We have now under our eye an original report, sent to the Regency by one of these commissioners, Herr Roesler (member for Oels), the contents of which are rather characteristic. It is dated, Stuttgart, June 30, 1849. After describing the adventures of half a dozen of these commissioners in a resultless search for cash, he gives a series of excuses for not having yet gone to his post, and then delivers himself of a most weighty argument respecting possible differences between Prussia, Austria, Bavaria, and Würtemberg, with their possible consequences. After having fully considered this, he comes, however, to the conclusion that there is no more chance. Next, he proposes to establish relays of trustworthy men for the conveyance of intelligence, and a system of espionage as to the intentions of the Würtemberg Ministry and the movements of the troops. This letter never reached its address, for when it was written the "Regency" had already passed entirely into the "foreign department," viz., Switzerland; and while poor Herr Roesler troubled his head about the intentions of the formidable ministry of a sixth-rate kingdom, a hundred thousand Prussian, Bavarian, and Hessian soldiers had already settled the whole affair in the last battle under the walls of Rastatt.

Thus vanished the German Parliament, and with it the first and last creation of the Revolution. Its convocation had been the first evidence that there actually *had been* a revolution in January; and it existed as long as this, the first modern German Revolution, was not yet brought to a close. Chosen under the influence of the capitalist class by a dismembered, scattered, rural population, for the most part only awaking from the dumbness of feudalism, this Parliament served to bring in one body upon the political arena all the great popular names of 1820-1848, and then to utterly ruin them. All the celebrities of middle class Liberalism were here collected. The bourgeoisie expected wonders; it earned shame for itself and its representatives. The industrial and commercial capitalist class were more severely defeated in Germany than in any other country; they were first worsted, broken, expelled from office in every individual State of Germany, and then put to rout, disgraced and hooted in the Central German Parliament. Political Liberalism, the rule of the bourgeoisie, be it under a Monarchical or Republican form of government, is forever impossible in Germany.

In the latter period of its existence, the German Parliament served to disgrace forever that section which had ever since March, 1848, headed the official opposition, the Democrats representing the interests of the small trading, and partially of the farming class. That class was, in May and June, 1849, given a chance to

show its means of forming a stable Government
in Germany. We have seen how it failed; not
so much by adverse circumstances as by the actual and continued cowardice in all trying movements that had occurred since the outbreak of
the revolution; by showing in politics the same
shortsighted, pusillanimous, wavering spirit,
which is characteristic of its commercial operations. In May, 1849, it had, by this course, lost
the confidence of the real fighting mass of all
European insurrections, the working class. But
yet, it had a fair chance. The German Parliament belonged to it, exclusively, after the Reactionists and Liberals had withdrawn. The rural
population was in its favor. Two-thirds of the
armies of the smaller States, one-third of the
Prussian army, the majority of the Prussian
Landwehr (reserve or militia), were ready to
join it, if it only acted resolutely, and with that
courage which is the result of a clear insight into the state of things. But the politicians who
led on this class were not more clear-sighted
than the host of petty tradesmen which followed
them. They proved even to be more infatuated,
more ardently attached to delusions voluntarily
kept up, more credulous, more incapable of resolutely dealing with facts than the Liberals. Their
political importance, too, is reduced below the
freezing-point. But not having actually carried
their common-place principles into execution,
they were, under *very* favorable circumstances,
capable of a momentary resurrection, when this
last hope was taken from them, just as it was

taken from their colleagues of the "pure Democracy" in France by the *coup d'etat* of Louis Bonaparte.

The defeat of the south-west German insurrection, and the dispersion of the German Parliament, bring the history of the first German insurrection to a close. We have now to cast a parting glance upon the victorious members of the counter-revolutionary alliance; we shall do this in our next letter. *

LONDON, September 24, 1852.

---

* After repeated search I have been unable to find the "next letter" referred to in the above paragraph; and, if it was ever written, there seems no doubt it was never published.—E. M. A.

XX.

THE LATE TRIAL AT COLOGNE.

December 22, 1852.

You will have ere this received by the European papers numerous reports of the Communist Monster Trial at Cologne, Prussia, and of its result. But as none of the reports is anything like a faithful statement of the facts, and as these facts throw a glaring light upon the political means by which the continent of Europe is kept in bondage, I consider it necessary to revert to this trial.

The Communist or Proletarian party, as well as other parties, had lost, by suppression of the rights of association and meeting, the means of giving to itself a legal organization on the Continent. Its leaders, besides, had been exiled from their countries. But no political party can exist without an organization; and that organization which both the Liberal bourgeois and the Democratic shopkeeping class were enabled more or less to supply by the social station, advantages, and long-established, every-day intercourse of their members, the proletarian class, without such social station and pecuniary means, was necessarily compelled to seek in secret association.   Hence, both in France and Germany, sprung up those numerous secret Societies which have, ever since 1849, one after another, been discovered by the police, and prosecuted as conspiracies; but if many of them were really conspiracies, formed with the actual intention of upsetting the Government for the time being, — and he is a coward that under certain circumstances would not conspire, just as he is a fool who, under other circumstances, would do so; — there were some other Societies which were formed with a wider and more elevated purpose, which knew that the upsetting of an existing Government was but a passing stage in the great impending struggle, and which intended to keep together and to prepare the party, whose nucleus they formed, for the last decisive combat which must, one day or another, crush forever in Europe the domination, not of mere "tyrants," "despots" and "usurpers," but of a power far superior, and far more formidable than theirs; that of capital over labor.

The organization of the advanced Communist party in Germany was of this kind. In accordance with the principles of the "Manifesto" * (published in 1848), and with those explained in the series of articles on "Revolution and

---

*) "The Manifesto." This is the celebrated "Communist Manifesto," which the Communist Congress, held in London, November, 1847, delegated Marx and Engels to draw up. It was published in 1848 (in London). The fundamental proposition of the Manifesto, Engels writes in his introduction to the "Communist Manifesto," translated by S. Moore,

Counter-Revolution in Germany," published in the *New York Daily Tribune,* this party never imagined itself capable of producing, at any time and at its pleasure, that revolution which was to carry its ideas into practice. It studied the causes that had produced the revolutionary movement in 1848, and the causes that made them fail. Recognizing the social antagonism of classes at the bottom of all political struggles, it applied itself to the study of the conditions under which one class of society can and must be called on to represent the whole of the interests of a nation, and thus politically to rule over it. History showed to the Communist party how, after the landed aristocracy of the Middle Ages, the monied power of the first capitalists arose and seized the

and published by W. Reeves, "is that in every historical epoch, the prevailing mode of economic production and exchange, and the social organization necessarily following from it, form the basis upon which is built up, and from which alone can be explained, the political and intellectual history of that epoch; that consequently the whole history of mankind has been a history of class struggles, contests between exploiting and exploited, ruling and oppressed classes; that nowadays a stage has been reached where the exploited and oppressed class—the proletariat—cannot attain its emancipation . . . without at the same time, and once and for all emancipating society at large from all exploitation, oppression, class distinctions, and class struggles." As to this fundamental propostion of the Manifesto, it "belongs," says Engels, "wholly and solely to Marx." The "Communist Manifesto" has been translated into well-nigh every language, and is, again to quote Engels, "the most international production of all Socialist literature."

reins of Government; how the social influence
and political rule of this financial section of capitalists was superseded by the rising strength
since the introduction of steam, of the manufacturing capitalists, and how at the present moment two more classes claim their turn of domination, the petty trading class and the industrial
working class. The practical revolutionary experience of 1848-1849 confirmed the reasonings
of theory, which led to the conclusion that the
Democracy of the petty traders must first have
its turn, before the Communist working class
could hope to permanently establish itself in
power and destroy that system of wage-slavery
which keeps it under the yoke of the bourgeoisie.
Thus the secret organization of the Communists
could not have the direct purpose of upsetting
the present Governments of Germany. Being
formed to upset not these, but the insurrectionary Government, which is sooner or later to follow them, its members might, and certainly
would, individually, lend an active hand to a
revolutionary movement against the present *status quo* in its turn; but the preparation of such
a movement, otherwise than by spreading of
Communist opinions by the masses, could not be
an object of the Association. So well was this
foundation of the Society understood by the
majority of its members, that when the place-
hunting ambition of some tried to turn it into a
conspiracy for making an extempore revolution,
they were speedily turned out.

Now, according to no law upon the face of
the earth, could such an Association be called

a plot, a conspiracy for purposes of high treason. If it was a conspiracy, it was one against, not the existing Government, but its probable successor. And the Prussian Government was aware of it. That was the cause why the eleven defendants were kept in solitary confinement during eighteen months, spent, on the part of the authorities, in the strangest judicial feats. Imagine, that after eight months' detention, the prisoners were remanded for some months more, "there being no evidence of any crime against them!" And when at last they were brought before a jury, there was not a single overt act of a treasonable nature proved against them. And yet they were convicted, and you will speedily see how.

One of the emissaries of the society was arrested in May, 1851, and from documents found upon him, other arrests followed. A Prussian police officer, a certain Stieber, was immediately ordered to trace the ramifications, in London, of the pretended plot. He succeeded in obtaining some papers connected with the above-mentioned seceders from the society, who had, after being turned out, formed an actual conspiracy in Paris and London. These papers were obtained by a double crime. A man named Reuter was bribed to break open the writing-desk of the secretary of the Society, and steal the papers therefrom. But that was nothing yet. This theft led to the discovery and conviction of the so-called Franco-German plot, in Paris, but it gave no clue as to the great Communist Association. The Paris plot, we may as well here observe, was under the direction of a few ambitious imbeciles and political *chevaliers d'industrie* in London, and of a formerly convicted forger, then acting as a police spy in Paris; their dupes made up, by rabid declamations and blood-thirsty rantings, for the utter insignificance of their political existence.

The Prussian police, then, had to look out for fresh discoveries. They established a regular office of secret police at the Prussian Embassy in London. A police agent, Greif by name, held his odious vocation under the title of an attaché to the Embassy — a step which should suffice to put all Prussian embassies out of the pale of international law, and which even the Austrians have not yet dared to take. Under him worked a certain Fleury, a merchant in the city of London, a man of some fortune and rather respectably connected, one of those low creatures who do the basest actions from an innate inclination to infamy. Another agent was a commercial clerk named Hirsch, who, however, had already been denounced as a spy on his arrival. He introduced himself into the society of some German Communist refugees in London, and they, in order to obtain proofs of his real character, admitted him for a short time. The proofs of his connection with the police were very soon obtained, and Herr Hirsch, from that time, absented himself. Although, however, he thus resigned all opportunities of gaining the information he was paid to procure, he was not inactive. From his retreat in Kensington, where he never met one of the Communists in question, he manufactured every week pretended reports of pretended sittings of a pretended Central Committee of that very conspiracy which the Prussian police could not get hold of. The contents of these reports were of the most absurd nature; not a Christian name was correct, not a name correctly spelt, not a single individual made to speak as he would be likely to speak. His master, Fleury, assisted him in this forgery, and it is not yet proved that "Attaché" Greif can wash his hands of these infamous proceedings. The Prussian Government, incredible to say, took these silly fabrications for gospel truth, and you may imagine what a confusion such depositions created in the evidence brought before the jury. When the trial came on, Herr Stieber, the already mentioned police officer, got into the witness-box, swore to all these absurdities, and, with no little self-complacency, maintained that he had a secret agent in the very closest intimacy with those parties in London who were considered the prime movers in this awful conspiracy. This secret agent was very secret indeed, for he had hid his face for eight months in Kensington, for fear he might actually see one of the parties whose most secret thoughts, words and doings, he pretended to report week after week.

Messrs. Hirsch and Fleury, however, had another invention in store. They worked up the whole of the reports they had made into an "original minute book" of the sittings of the Secret Supreme Committee, whose existence was maintained by the Prussian police; and Herr Stieber, finding that this book wondrously agreed with

the reports already received from the same parties, at once laid it before the jury, declaring
upon his oath that after serious examination, and
according to his fullest conviction, that book
was genuine. It was then that most of the absurdities reported by Hirsch were made public.
You may imagine the surprise of the pretended
members of that Secret Committee when they
found things stated of them which they never
knew before. Some who were baptized William
were here christened Louis or Charles; others,
at the time they were at the other end of England, were made to have pronounced speeches in
London; others were reported to have read letters they never had received; they were made to
have met regularly on a Thursday, when they
used to have a convivial reunion, once a week, on
Wednesdays; a working man, who could hardly
write, figured as one of the takers of minutes,
and signed as such; and they all of them were
made to speak in a language which, if it may be
that of Prussian police stations, was certainly not
that of a reunion in which literary men, favorably
known in their country, formed the majority.
And, to crown the whole, a receipt was forged
for a sum of money, pretended to have been paid
by the fabricators to the pretended secretary of
the fictitious Central Committee for this book;
but the existence of this pretended secretary
rested merely upon a hoax that some malicious
Communist had played upon the unfortunate
Hirsch.

This clumsy fabrication was too scandalous an
affair not to produce the contrary of its intended

effect. Although the London friends of the defendants were deprived of all means to bring the facts of the case before the jury — although the letters they sent to the counsel for the defence were suppressed by the post — although the documents and affidavits they succeeded in getting into the hands of these legal gentlemen were not admitted in evidence, yet the general indignation was such that even the public accusers, nay, even Herr Stieber — whose oath had been given as a guarantee for the authenticity of that book — were compelled to recognize it as a forgery.

This forgery, however, was not the only thing of the kind of which the police was guilty. Two or three more cases of the sort came out during the trial. The documents stolen by Reuter were interpolated by the police so as to disfigure their meaning. A paper, containing some rabid nonsense, was written in a handwriting imitating that of Dr. Marx, and for a time it was pretended that it had been written by him, until at last the prosecution was obliged to acknowledge the forgery. But for every police infamy that was proved as such, there were five or six fresh ones brought forward, which could not, at the moment, be unveiled, the defence being taken by surprise, the proofs having to be got from London, and every correspondence of the counsel for the defence with the London Communist refugees being in open court treated as complicity in the alleged plot!

That Greif and Fleury are what they are here represented to be has been stated by Herr Stieber himself, in his evidence; as to Hirsch, he has before a London magistrate confessed that he forged the "minute book," by order and with the assistance of Fleury, and then made his escape from this country in order to evade a criminal prosecution.

The Government could stand few such branding disclosures as came to light during the trial. It had a jury — six nobles, two Government officials. These were not the men to look closely into the confused mass of evidence heaped before them during six weeks, when they heard it continually dinned into their ears that the defendants were the chiefs of a dreadful Communist conspiracy, got up in order to subvert everything sacred — property, family, religion, order, government and law! And yet, had not the Government, at the same time, brought it to the knowledge of the privileged classes, that an acquittal in this trial would be the signal for the suppression of the jury; and that it would be taken as a direct political demonstration — as a proof of the middle-class Liberal Opposition being ready to unite even with the most extreme revolutionists — the verdict would have been an acquittal. As it was, the retroactive application of the new Prussian code enabled the Government to have seven prisoners convicted, while four merely were acquitted, and those convicted were sentenced to imprisonment varying from three to six years, as you have, doubtless, already stated at the time the news reached you.

LONDON, December 1, 1852.

CPSIA information can be obtained
at www.ICGtesting.com
Printed in the USA
LVHW032351090322
712957LV00002B/220

9 781614 276326